The MILLENNIUM AND BEYOND

The Prophecies, Your Potential

TERESA MOOREY

Hodder & Stoughton

A MEMBER OF THE HODDER HEADLINE GROUP

Dedication

For all that is best, in each of us

Order queries: please contact Bookpoint Ltd, 39 Milton Park, Abingdon, Oxon OX14 4TD. Telephone: (44) 01235 400414, Fax: (44) 01235 400454. Lines are open from 9.00–6.00, Monday to Saturday, with a 24-hour message answering service.
Email address: orders@bookpoint.co.uk

British Library Cataloguing in Publication Data
A catalogue record for this title is available from The British Library

ISBN 0 340 72449 8

First published 1999
Impression number 10 9 8 7 6 5 4 3 2 1
Year 2003 2002 2001 2000 1999

Text illustrations by Jane Brideson and David Hancock
Cover illustration by Jacey/represented by Début Art

Typeset by Transet Limited, Coventry, England.
Printed in Great Britain for Hodder & Stoughton Educational, a division of Hodder Headline plc, 338 Euston Road, London NW1 3BH by Cox & Wyman, Reading, Berkshire.

CONTENTS

Acknowledgements

Grateful thanks to my friend, Steve Eddy, for advice and help with this book and others. Very special thanks to Steve and his co-author, Nicholas Campion, for allowing me a preview of pages from their book *A New Astrology: The Art and Science of the Heavens* to be published by Bloomsbury, 1999. This has been of immense help to me.

Many thanks to David Elkington, writer, Egyptologist and mythographer, for his help and for a glimpse into his forthcoming work, *Jesus BC* to be published in the spring of 1999 through Curtis Brown. Acknowledgements also to the agents Curtis Brown.

Thanks also to John Burford, numerologist, author and friend of mine, for the advice and material he has given to me.

Thanks to Bob Frissell and Frog Ltd for permission to use their material.

Also by the same author

The Moon and You for Beginners

Witchcraft – A Beginner's Guide

Paganism – A Beginner's Guide

Herbs for Magic and Ritual – A Beginner's Guide

Shamanism – A Beginner's Guide

The Goddess – A Beginner's Guide

Earth Mysteries – A Beginner's Guide

The Magic and Mystery of Trees – A Beginner's Guide

Ghosts – A Beginner's Guide

Sex Signs – A Beginner's Guide

Spells and Rituals – A Beginner's Guide

Pagan Gods for Today's Man – A Beginner's Guide (with Howard Moorey)

The Wheel of the Year – Myth and Magic Through the Seasons (with Jane Brideson)

Reach Your Potential – a series of 12 books, one for each of the signs of the zodiac

Note: In this book the terms CE (Common Era) and BCE (Before Common Era) are used, in place of the more usual AD and BC.

1 THE DOOR OPENS

You would measure time the measureless and
the immeasurable...
Yet the timeless in you is aware of life's
timelessness,
And knows that yesterday is but today's
memory and tomorrow is today's dream.

KAHLIL GIBRAN, *THE PROPHET*

Our entrance into the twenty-first century feels like an awesome step. Life, for some of us, has never offered so many options. I do not refer to economic and technological advancement, for that does not benefit everyone, even in the Western world. I mean, rather, we have conceptual freedoms. We are able to think for ourselves in ways undreamed of, even 50 years ago. In other respects the times have never been so fearful. Like a plane approaching the sound barrier, whispered anxieties and echoing prophecies build up along our flight path and we are waiting for some kind of bang. Will it arrive in the year 2000? Or in 2001, when some say the new millennium really begins? Or in the year 2012, as the Mayan prophecy may indicate? Possibly the year of reckoning will be even later. Thursday, 26 October 2028 has been given by some scientists as Doomsday Date, when asteroid 1997 XF11 passes too close to the earth for comfort. Do we really face disaster from some source, or do the times offer us an opportunity for a radical advancement in human consciousness? Since scientists split the atom our world has not felt safe – indeed it has not been safe. Now there are many more threats, both manmade, in the shape of pollution, global warming, etc., and natural such as huge earthquakes and poleshift. The year 2000 is certainly a threat to our computer systems, for many are date-dependent and not programmed for three noughts, and unless put right this may affect almost everything – hospitals, banks, supermarkets, air-traffic control. In short, every corner of modern life. Some people acknowledge they fear massive catastrophe, a few expect messiahs or the Antichrist. Others feel uneasy, or merely curious.

Two keywords for our age seem to be 'fear' and 'freedom'. Our fears arise because our knowledge has effectively outstripped our wisdom. From atomic fusion to the cloning of sheep, science is taking us into realms for which we have not had time to formulate an ethical perspective. Professor Stephen Hawking, speaking in the White House, Washington DC, in the spring of 1998, stated that human genetic engineering cannot be stopped and is likely to happen in the next millennium, whether most of us want it or not. Our old dogmas no longer insulate us against such challenges and few new ones are emerging. We think for ourselves, but mostly we have not learnt to do this positively and creatively. We are preoccupied with facts rather than meanings and, rather than having our sense of direction enhanced, we feel out of control. In *From Atlantis to the Sphinx* (see Further Reading) Colin Wilson makes the following point:

> *As man ceased to be mere animal, he ceased to be passive. He began to feel there was something he could do to CONTROL the world in which he found himself. At first, this attempt at control came through various forms of ritual . . . 'True man' is a religious animal.*

However, while ancient people attempted to control their environment in a variety of ways, some of which we could, indeed, term religious, these people, by many accounts, felt themselves to be a part of that which they sought to direct. What happened in the individual happened in the collective, and vice versa. Human spirit was contained within the Great Spirit and the Great Spirit moved within land, sea and sky. Any 'control' was more a case of steering a boat on the current, rather that attempting to navigate upstream. Some may term this state of primeval participation in nature 'primitive'; others regard it as a Golden Age. A more scientific explanation may be that in times past humans possessed a greater 'right brain' consciousness.

OUR SPLIT BRAINS

The human brain is divided into two hemispheres, the right and the left. The left brain controls the right side of the body, the right brain the left side of the body, so each has a foot in the other's camp, so to speak. However, these hemispheres are concerned with different functions. The left brain is the home of reasoning and logical thought, while the right perceives patterns, recognises faces, appreciates art. (This is reversed in left-handed people.) Again, to quote Colin Wilson '. . . you could say that the left is a scientist and the right is an artist'. While these two sides are connected by a bridge of nerves called the corpus callosum, the part of each of us that says 'I am' lives in the left side.

However, someone else speaks to us from the other side when we are inspired, creative or deeply relaxed. Maybe you have sometimes felt there was another 'you' inside, at once older and wiser, yet relaxed and playful? This may be your apprehension of your 'right-brain' consciousness.

In *The Origin of Consciousness in the Breakdown of the Bicameral Mind* (1976) the psychologist Julian Jaynes put forward the theory that in times past humans were much more influenced by their right brain. Ancient Greek, Sumerian and biblical heroes often heard voices, which they interpreted as being those of the gods, but were, in fact, communications from their own right brain (the question here is begged about what God/gods may be and whether the 'right brain' is more connected to this source). These heroes have no personal life or perspective, no inner mind space from which to survey the world. They do not seem conscious of their own awareness. Perhaps we could say they were a part of that which they perceived. According to Jaynes this stage of affairs continued until as recently as about 1250 BCE. Then, as the Bronze Age gave way to the Iron Age, conquest and cruelty entered upon the human stage, following upon the sense of alienation that now pervaded. The voices of the ancestors were silent. The gods had departed from stream, woodland and mountainside. Human beings were 'ghosts in the machine' of their own bodies, cold and alone, severed from that all-pervading unity that had been home. Could this be the real meaning of the 'Fall'? We have compensated for this by ever-greater feats of conquest and, because of this, fear has been our legacy. Most of us have some unspoken agenda of competition which makes us a threat, to a greater or lesser extent, to others of our species and while we are apt to call this the law of life, or the law of the jungle, no other animals can compete with us for cruelty to our own kind. Our conquest of Nature has been our consolation prize. It may be time to look to our laurels.

DOOMSDAY CULTS AND FEARS

One response to the atmosphere of fear has been a growth in Doomsday cults, which are no doubt an intense, localised manifestation of impulses that have been with us for centuries. These groups can be defined as a type of mind-control cult, tightly controlling the behaviour, thoughts and even emotions of the members. Doomsday cults usually hold apocalyptic beliefs, that is, they believe that some dread Day of Judgment, as foretold in the Bible, is at hand, and that only an elite will be saved. Group suicide may be embraced as a means to evade the coming destruction and to be transported, all at once, to a Heavenly abode, later to play a key role when the 'end of time' arrives. Other more general distinguishing features include leadership by a single dominant and charismatic male, who often commands whatever sexual favours he wishes; the members tend to live together in a small and isolated community; information from outside the cult is severely restricted and there is an atmosphere of paranoia; the religious beliefs of the group are not those of an established denomination, although there may be resemblances; members become isolated from their families and there is usually a lack of sound information as to the beliefs of the cult. Apart from the final two points, such cults are little more than extremely dogmatic and fundamentalist forms of religion.

It is not hard to see how such groups might appeal, not only to the 'weak-minded' but to anyone going through crisis or who is otherwise especially vulnerable, for they offer a haven from the malaise of our times, even though this haven may be temporary, or even dangerous. Their chief gift is that sense of 'belonging' for which we all hanker and have hankered, probably for millennia. Sexual undertones only heighten this, for sex is another way of achieving 'belonging'. Control is another factor. By defining themselves as an elite and even by electing mass suicide, some 'control' is felt to be achieved in a world that has never felt so out of control. Any leader who opts for complete control usually directs the sexuality of the members, for sex is a powerful force that will in some way threaten the position of many an autocrat, if it is not kept on a leash.

The majority of us who have never been touched by the influence of any cult, or similar, should perhaps not feel that we are free from the forces involved, for we are all searching for a 'home', and we are all, to some extent, paranoid. We see things outside us and fear them, when these are distorted and exaggerated images of that within us, which we fear. This is vastly different, of course, from the medical condition of paranoia, and is not necessarily quite the same as the casual remark often thrown at anyone who seems to have irrational fears, 'Oh, you're just paranoid!' However, it all adds up to the same thing essentially. We all fear bits of ourselves and instead of sorting this out we project our fear, hatred or dislike outwards, choosing instead to dislike something that is not part of us because it is naturally more comfortable. Perhaps there is something you are afraid of, or hate, out of all proportion to its proven ability to inflict real harm upon you? If so, welcome to the human race! As citizens of the twenty-first century, one of our tasks should perhaps be to examine anything that we hate and fear in the light of our own inner demons. Of course, there are things that are naturally hateful and fearful, but whence comes that 'edge', that power, that certain things possess to terrify or enrage?

We encounter this idea again in the section on 'The shadow', in Chapter 8. Suffice to say, for the moment, that what we detest says more about what is inside us than what is outside, for we tend to 'project', or externalise elements within us that we find unacceptable. If we have an especial dislike for 'loudmouths', it is unpalatable, to say the least, to entertain the idea that this may be because we have a denied Motormouth inside, longing to get out. This is another example of alienation from self, an absence of unity, an interior split that may also be connected with right/left brain duality, for it is hard to imagine our instinctual selves raising such rigid discriminations. But it is not only the undesirable that we deny and externalise, for we often repress our special qualities too, fearing our own power. So what we have here is an invitation to look inwards as well as outwards, to be quick to question, slow to take up a position of self-righteousness, to think in terms of understanding, kinship, unity, rather than polarising with good/bad, right/wrong. It is also an invitation to look at why we fear the future and the early years of the twenty-first century, if we do. Are we afraid of change? Are we afraid of our own powers to make huge changes and how that might rock our little world? But what if these changes are changes for the better . . . ?

MILLENARIAN FEAR

Millenarian fear is not new. Around 600 BCE what has been termed a growth in consciousness in the human race appears to have crystallised in the shape of philosophers and religious founders, such as Buddha, Confucius, Lao Tzu, Pythagoras and Zoroaster. This has been hailed by historians as an advancement, but may rather have been inspired effort by persons of outstanding spirit, to preserve what might otherwise be lost, to enable the human race, now travelling into the barren lands of left-brain logic to take with them the balm of unity consciousness. We have seen that it is probable that early humans lived in a kind of Dreamtime, feeling at one with Creation, possibly with highly developed intuitive faculties – call this 'right-brain' consciousness, mystical participation or by any other name. As time advanced, logic and the development of ego-consciousness (i.e. the principal sense of oneself as an individual) became paramount, bringing with it an attitude of conquest and violence. The Chinese seer, Lao Tzu tells us

The way that can be spoken of
Is not the constant way;
The name that can be named
Is not the constant name

TAO TE CHING

Was this the philosopher's way of saying that what is truly valuable and meaningful cannot be encompassed by logic? Such things feel like a 'revelation' when they impinge upon our normal consciousness, but they are ordinary stuff to the right half of the brain. And were Lao Tzu and others of his ilk seeking to preserve an ember of what had once been the fires of human spirituality? In other words, was he articulating something that was dying, that always dies in part when put into words and which the human race has been struggling for the lack of – a living connection with the cosmos? The inspirations of Lao Tzu and the Buddha may have been those of minds who possessed both the gifts of clear and objective thought in addition to the fading faculty of intuition and perception of divine totality, that was once the birthright of all.

The advent of the prophet Zoroaster marked the end of the concept of time as cyclical, the ever-repeating rhythms of the Dreamtime, and gave birth, in effect, to Millenarianism. The rational side of the brain loves clear distinctions and, with Zoroastrianism, the idea of a dual universe of battling good and evil gained ground, bringing with it the vision of a final conflict, an end-of-time apocalypse when evil is at last cast down and the 'chosen' inherit the Kingdom. The instinctual mind is more at home with the idea of time as a cycle, ever returning in circles and spirals, changing yet enduring. The logical, alienated self thinks in terms of endings and beginnings, time as linear. Linear time has an end and that end is visualised as Armaggedon. In a sense, our conscious minds are prisoners of time. Its relentless march is depressing, but the instinctual self perceives time differently, as a totality or as an open dimension. It seems that at some level we know that our concept of time is deficient, hence time travel is a favourite sci-fi theme, involving, as it does, mind-blowing paradoxes and convolutions.

CONCEPTS OF TIME

The twenty-first century is our concept. Even if we are literal about accepting the Christian story, it is still unlikely that the birth of the historical Christ took place in 1 AD, or 0 AD. (Actually, only one in six people link the millennium in any way to the birth of Christ.) The fact that it is our concept does not destroy its importance, for to a great extent we create our own reality – an idea we shall be encountering again later. However, it is important to bear in mind that it is our counting system that has produced this significant date.

The ancient view of time was relative, in many cultures depending on the mood of the gods. Time and space were interdependent in countries which possessed advanced mathematical systems, for example Egypt, India and Babylon. The here and now was often conceived as existing alongside a transcendent, eternal time, such as Plato's world of perfect forms, or the Dreamtime of the Aborigines. Certain native peoples still retain this fluid impression of time. For instance, the Hopi Indians live in what amounts to an eternal present, the Hopi language contains no word for time and no tenses. Buddhists regard this as the world of *maya* or illusion and, by this token, time, as we perceive it, is also illusory. Around 750 BCE the Greek poet Hesiod suggested that it might be possible for time to flow backwards, and that in the golden age people might grow younger as time passed. One of the Maya records gives a date of 10,240,000,000,000 years ago which one Mayan expert, Jose Arguelles, has jokingly described as so far back it's probably in the future – an intriguing idea that gives us pause, for no logical reason. The idea of a 'clockwork universe' and time as a mathematically fixed constant was taught by Isaac Newton (although Newton was, in fact, of a strongly mystical bent and performed his scientific feats almost in his spare time). However, Einstein's physics brings a totally different perspective and one to which we have not popularly adapted. In a sense, Einstein's relative universe harks back to ancient ideas of space and time.

To the person in the street the universe is still thought of as 'clockwork'. However, Einstein held that all motion is relative, i.e. something 'moves' only in relation to other subjects, not essentially. Time being measured by movement is therefore also relative; one of Einstein's definitions states 'time is a property of matter in motion'. The general theory of relativity includes the belief that time stands still at the speed of light, so, as an example, an astronaut going off on a 20-year journey at 99.9 per cent of the speed of light would come back to earth 10,000 earth years later, to find friends and family departed into the dim corridors of history. This fact has been proved through comparing the time on two atomic clocks, one of which is flown around the world at high speed and can be shown to have fallen minutely behind its counterpart, left in its original position. Modern physics now seriously considers the possible existence of an infinite number of parallel universes, which could make time travel possible without running into paradoxes, such as the possibility of preventing one's own birth. But perhaps one *could* prevent one's own birth . . . Here we enter the realms beloved of science fiction, that may soon become science fact.

We are limited in our investigation of time by the fact that we apparently move steadily through it, without being conscious of our motion. Someone who lived and died on a conveyor belt, wearing blinkers, with head held in a vice facing forwards, would have a most distorted view of his surroundings and, while this is a most inadequate analogy, perhaps our movement through time creates a similarly erroneous picture. We think of the possibility of going backwards or forwards in time, but if time is a cycle, it may be more a question of jumping to the next loop of the spiral. Or perhaps time is more like an ocean, with tides and currents. Time to us is like the relentless march of a destructive robot, and we spend our lives battling against the clock. However, like many things, it is possible that our concepts of time are limited and defective, and that we are erecting our own barriers.

THE ANCIENT GREAT YEAR AND MODERN COSMOLOGY

Existence can be seen as cycles within cycles, human life associated with the life–death cycle of the seasons, the rising and setting of the sun in its daily round paralleling its yearly approach and departure as summer is followed by winter. Each month the moon passes from new to full and back again to new. By this transformation, implying rebirth after dissolution and promoting faith in the process of life, humans may have been encouraged to think in the abstract, for the moon presumably continues to exist even when not visible. Interest in measurement of celestial cycles is extremely ancient, predating settled life, and by about 3000 BCE, the time of the building of the great stone circles, astronomical patterns were noted with a sophistication we are only beginning to appreciate. Greater cycles were postulated, within the universe, within which the observed cycles were 'held' and which were larger versions of the smaller periods.

The Babylonian ritual year of 360 days gave rise to the 'Great Year' known as a 'Sar', lasting 3,600 years. The Babylonians bequeathed to the Assyrians a complex system of timekeeping, designed to measure time both cyclical and sacred, from the smallest to the greatest. Their Great Year was based on symbolic figures, reflecting belief that planetary cycles moved in harmony with terrestrial cycles.

The smallest Assyrian unit consisted of one human breath, i.e. 4 seconds. This measurement implied belief that the universe is a living, breathing system. The system grew through a 4-minute period, a 2-hour period, up to a day, a decan (10 days), a 30-day month, a 360-day 'year' and so on to larger periods, mathematically compiled and designed to measure the life of the universe. A Soss was 60 years, a Ner 600 years, a Sar of 3,600 years and a Great Sar of 216,000 years (i.e. 60 to the power of 3), this latter constituting one 'in-breath'. As out-breath must follow in-breath, the total life of the universe was held to be 432,000 years. A still larger mythic period consisted of 12,960,000 years. We may feel that this is fanciful and irrelevant to us, but it contains the important supposition that the human is part of a greater plan, and central to the universe, and that both are cyclical.

The idea that the universe evolved in order to allow humans to exist is gaining popularity with astronomers. Some astronomers believe that the inherent tendency for chaos to resolve itself within the universe, into galaxies and star systems, indicates that there is a purpose at work behind it all. Even more noteworthy is the fact that conditions have evolved that are conducive to life, for the odds against this happening by chance are immense. If certain conditions involved in the Big Bang (see below), such as gravity or nuclear force, were even fractionally different, life could not have come to exist. It hardly seems we are here 'by accident', but rather that there is some grand plan at work, to which the existence of human beings is central. Some astronomers indeed believe that the universe would not exist without intelligent life to observe it. This 'Anthropic Principle' explored by Gribbin and Rees in *The Stuff of the Universe* (Heinemann, 1990) effectively restores humanity to the centre of the universe and may be the most radical theory within modern astronomy. One form of the Anthropic Principle states that intelligent life is an inevitable outcome of the evolution of the universe and once created it can never die out. Almost, the cosmos becomes a product of the human imagination similar to the Dreamtime of the Aborigines.

Other concepts of the Great Year include the Precessional Year or Precessional Cycle, explained in Chapter 2, 'The Age of Aquarius', and the Hindu idea of the Yugas. The Hindu basic unit of mythical time is the Maha Yuga of 4,320,000 years, comprised of a Golden Age or Krtiayuga of 1,728,000, a Silver Age (Tretayuga) of 1,296,000 years, a Copper Age of 864,000 years (Dvaparayuga) and the current Earthen Age of 432,000, the Kaliyuga. This is the reign of the Mother Goddess, Kali, who is known as a destructive figure. However, we also know that the Dark Goddess, in whatever guise she comes, destroys in order to give birth once more.

A different definition of the Kali Yuga is given by Bob Frissell (see Further Reading). In this system the Kali Yuga lasts 2,000 years, comprising one-twelfth of the precessional cycle. Precession is caused by a wobble of the earth on its axis, meaning that the North Pole projected into space, traces a slow ellipse, pointing every 25,920 years (approximately) towards the centre of the galaxy, and then moving away, only to return once more as the cycle develops. This cycle is like a vastly extended version of day and night. As we move away from the galactic centre we 'fall asleep' and consciousness drops in humanity. As we turn and move towards the centre, we start to 'wake up'. Currently, we are at this turning point, starting to wake up, and this stage of the cycle is also called the Kali Yuga. For the last 2,000 years we have been 'asleep'. Frissell writes:

> *. . . so almost everything written about the cosmic cycle in the last 2,000 years was interpreted by people asleep trying to extract from ancient writings they didn't even understand . . . In other words, most of the information is not very trustworthy.*
>
> *The ancients discovered two points located 900 years on either side of where we fall asleep and where we wake up. These points are each associated with tremendous change – changes of consciousness of beings . . .*
>
> *We sit now right at the turning point of beginning to move back toward the centre of the galaxy and start waking up . . .'*

Definition of the Maha Yuga as 4,320,000 years appears in the Hindu hymns called the *Vedas*, which are the equivalent of the book of Genesis in the Bible and are possibly the oldest literature in the world. However we measure them, the Hindu and similar systems consist of cycles within cycles, to infinity, for the Maha Yuga is only one-thousandth of a kalpa, or Day of Brahma, and so on. The entire structure rests on a Divine Year of 360 ordinary years; 360 years is assumed to be one year in the life of a soul. Thus, the underlying belief concerns the development of the human spirit in accordance with celestial cycles.

The timescales envisaged by peoples whom we might term 'primitive' are huge. A kalpa, as defined above, consists of 4,320 million years. In a sense the exact sum matters little, for the extent is unimaginable, and in any case, a kalpa is by no means the final figure, for a kalpa is only a day of Brahma, who lives for many years and then experiences successive incarnations. The important points are that time is conceived as cycles within cycles in a cosmic heartbeat and that the extent of time measured is incredibly immense. Fritjof Capra, the physicist, wrote that 'The scale of this ancient myth is indeed staggering; it has taken the human mind more than two thousand years to come up again with a similar concept.' Capra's remark refers to the theory of the pulsating universe, an extension of the well-known Big Bang theory.

The original Big Bang theory as outlined by G.E Lemaitre, the Belgian astronomer, postulates that at the beginning matter and energy were compressed into a 'cosmic egg' – a figure actually encountered in many ancient mythologies. This then grew rapidly or exploded outwards, sending out matter and energy in all directions and evolving into the still-expanding universe that we inhabit. A refinement of the Big Bang theory suggests that the universe will at some point cease to expand, beginning instead to contract until all matter collapses in upon itself to form an unimaginably dense core, creating immense heat until it creates another Big Bang and everything begins all over again. This sounds very much like Assyrian ideas of the universe breathing in and out. Science and ancient myth seem to be coming together. It does seem that our logical selves are working their way forwards (or perhaps backwards) to achieve a new understanding of what many have believed for so long – that the universe possesses sentience, pattern and meaning, and that our place in it is unique. Could this presage a new union between our 'dreamtime' selves and our conscious, reasoning part? This may well be the challenge of our times.

THE FREEDOM TO QUESTION

Fear and freedom were mentioned at the start of this chapter as two keywords for our times. It is rather paradoxical that, in the Western world, freed from so many chores by our technology, we rarely feel we have time to think. Despite the fact that we all tend to rush around like Lewis Carroll's White Rabbit, saying 'I'm late', we do actually have time to reflect and question that earlier generations did not enjoy. As recently as the 1950s, women were preoccupied with keeping their houses in apple-pie order. There isn't much energy to spare for pondering the 'nature of life and the purpose of existence' if you are busy polishing table-tops until you can see your face in them, or washing, starching and ironing for a family. The lives of men were likewise comparatively hard and physically exhausting. Technology has generally changed all of that, while standards also have altered, liberating us from some pointless striving. Of course, many of us have demanding lives and fears of joblessness keep many people at work well into 'playtime'. None the less, if we choose to use our time in this way we can reflect – while the toaster makes our toast, or while we are stuck in a traffic jam. More than this, we are *invited* to reflect. Information technology and the media put us in touch with limitless information and encourage us to form opinions on what would have seemed unthinkable earlier this century and during many previous centuries. There exists now a self-questioning climate, which is what the 'alternative scene' is concerned with, chiefly. If we have progressed through the mystical and instinctual (also called the right brain) into the logical and discriminatory, what might be our next step? Could it be a union of these two faculties, or something more?

The important point here, I feel, is that we do ask questions, that we go on asking questions and that we are not too addicted to finding the crystalline answer to our questions, that curtails our quest and enables us to settle back into our armchairs, self-satisfied and stagnant. One could say that it is not finding answers that is paramount, but asking the right questions. Our intellects aren't really happy with this. Reason says 'There must be a logical answer, so let's find it and be done with it'. However, once we think we have found an answer, we stop growing, we close down.

Myths often encode significant messages. An Arthurian myth, to which I often resort as an example, tells the story of the knight Parsifal on his quest for the Holy Grail. On his adventures, Parsifal found himself in a strange castle where a king was sick and a mysterious procession occurred involving a maiden carrying a chalice, or Grail. Like all the best heroes, Parsifal presumed his main function was gung-ho swordsmanship and, as there seemed no opportunity for this, he kept quiet. Whereupon the castle and all its inmates disappeared, leaving Parsifal alone. Left to wander and search for many years, Parsifal again found the castle and again saw the strange procession. Now older and much wiser, Parsifal lifts his voice and *asks* 'What is all this about? Why are you ill? What is the Grail for?' Magically, the sick king is healed and Parsifal discovers that he is heir to the kingdom. We need to note here that Parsifal does not receive a complex answer in triplicate, he receives the 'kingdom', which probably means he becomes truly lord over himself and his life, as much as anything. This story illustrates the importance of asking, even in those situations where we seemingly can't do anything about anything, and our 'swords' which may be our available tools and skills or the cutting edges of our intellects, are of no apparent use.

Our entry into the twenty-first century is the cue to ask questions – lots of them. Perhaps our favourite phrase could be 'What if . . . ?'

2

THE AGE OF AQUARIUS

No man can reveal to you aught but that which already lies half asleep in the dawning of your knowledge . . .

For the vision of one man lends not its wings to another man.

And even as each one of you stands alone in God's knowledge, so must each one of you be alone in his knowledge of God and his understanding of the earth.

KAHLIL GIBRAN, *THE PROPHET*

In the Flower Power era of the late 1960s a song from the hit rock musical *Hair* popularised the dawning of the Age of Aquarius, as a time of mystic crystal revelations and the mind's true liberation'. As a trendy idea, this has gone distinctly off the boil. However, the 'Age of Aquarius' is still on people's lips, and many of those who are even mildly aware that we may be on the threshold of momentous change use the phrase as if to conjure a new Utopia. So what is this 'Age of Aquarius' all about?

ASTROLOGICAL CONTEXT

To understand how this concept arises we have to know something about astrology and also some basic astronomy, because the Age of Aquarius depends upon celestial movements and astrology is the art of interpreting these in terms of terrestrial manifestation. The key phrase here is 'As above, so below', reputedly uttered by the ancient Egyptian sage Hermes Trismegistus, also called Thoth. This means that the placements of sun, moon and planets, in areas of the sky and relative to each other are connected to events on earth and to specific characteristics and events in the lives of individuals. Most astrologers do not imagine that the planets actually cause things to happen, but rather that they are 'synchronistic' so the connection here is something other than cause and effect. This may be difficult to understand and astrology is often scorned by the scientific establishment and even regarded as dangerous by some, for reasons which I do not understand, other than the fact that people are prone to find anything that challenges their cherished beliefs dangerous, at least to their own peace of mind! However, astrology has an impressive pedigree, arising from the very dawn of human consciousness, when lunar phases were notched on stone, through the classical era and the court astrologers of medieval times into our modern age, when the frontiers of science are expanding to suggest a universe that has sentience.

More specific studies also provide back-up for astrology. For instance, the statistical work of the astrologer Jeff Mayo supports some sun-sign interpretations, the French statistician Michel Gauquelin established a relationship between to position of certain planets and professional prominence, in line with traditional interpretation, and other work on the fringes of science, such as Maurice

Cotterell's studies of the solar wind (mentioned in Chapter 5) also lend weight to the old beliefs. As they say 'There is something in it'.

Proper astrology, for an individual, is based on the entire birth chart, drawn up for the place, date and time of birth, thus taking into account the positions of all of the planets, not just the sun (for the 'sign you were born under' or your 'star sign' is in fact the sign occupied by the sun when you were born). Thus astrology is extremely complex and involves a great deal more than reading you stars in a tabloid newspaper. However, having practised astrology for more than twenty years I have become increasingly aware of how people are like their sun sign – something which one scorns as being too simplistic as one begins to learn about true astrology. Of course, we are all infinitely complex, but the sun sign seems to provide the background colouring to the personality and sun-sign columns do at least keep a general awareness of astrology alive. The majority of astrologers are minimally concerned with how astrology works; they merely point to results, for with a reasonable amount of expertise astrology can be seen to work. To see astrology in action, you need, of course, to examine it, and so many astrologers can, with justification, answer critics with Isaac Newton's immortal response to Halley, on the same subject: 'I have studied it, sir. You have not.' Yes, that giant intellect that shaped much of our scientific thought was also interested in astrology.

An individual horoscope interprets, among other things, the placements of the planets in signs. The planets represent specific energies, the sign placement shows how this energy is likely to be expressed. Thus if you were born with Mars, the planet of assertion and fighting spirit, in the Fire sign Aries you are likely to be more forthright and aggressive than if it were placed in the defensive Water sign, Cancer. The birth chart is a freeze-frame that impinges upon, or describes the character of the individual. However, the planets are continually in motion, as cycle follows cycle and trends in the world in general are indicated, to some extent, by the movements of the planets from sign to sign, in the heavens. The movements of the outer planets, Uranus, Neptune and Pluto, are especially important in this respect.

THE OUTER PLANETS

Traditional astrology was based on the 'visible planets', Mercury, Venus, Mars, Jupiter and Saturn plus the 'luminaries', i.e. the sun and the moon. The extra-Saturnian planets, that is those orbiting beyond Saturn, were not discovered until comparatively recently. Of course, they were always there and always relevant, as present-day studies of horoscopes of royal persons from centuries past reveal. Their discovery heralds the emergence into consciousness of the themes they represent and seems to coincide, at least in regard to the Western world, with related events.

Uranus, in astrological terms, represents change, independence and self-reliance. It was discovered in 1781, by William Herschel, after whom the planet was initially named. This coincided with a period of upheaval and rebellion, for instance the French Revolution and American Independence. Uranus, or Ouranus, was the original sky god of the Greeks, who coupled with the earth to bring forth creation. We associate the sky with unpredictable change, lightning flashes and storms, and we also link it with mental processes, as we connect the earth with our bodies. Astrology is based on observed effects and it is intriguing how the outer planets have been named so appropriately. Uranus, named after the creator sky-god is the planet of independent and creative thought, of the

wide and clear vision that encompasses the landscape and ignores the sacred cows. In many ways it shows itself as a smasher of idols.

Neptune stands for our ability to dream dreams, create visions and to seek ideals. It may also mean confusion and loss of ego-consciousness. It was discovered in 1846 by Urbain Leverrier at a time when there was a surge of interest in the occult and all matters spiritual. Mesmerism, now known as hypnosis, was being experimented with and anaesthetics were introduced for pain relief. In addition charitable concern for orphans, the sick and needy was resulting in the establishment of homes and institutions. Neptune was the Greek god of the all-encompassing but fathomless ocean, dissolving boundaries, bringing about a 'sea change'. Neptune has a glamorous quality. It may promise the Garden of Eden, but it can lead to a quagmire. Neptune reveals other dimensions and creates beauty, love, charity and works of art, but it can also lead to chaos.

Pluto is the most recently discovered of the planets and, while it usually orbits furthest from the sun, at present it is inside the orbit of Neptune. This has given rise to some concern, for Pluto is perhaps the 'scariest' of the planets and there have been fears that with Pluto closer to the earth Plutonic effects would be strengthened. In addition, Pluto inhabited its own sign, Scorpio (i.e. the sign which it is said to rule, or be strongest in) from 1984 to 1996. Pluto is the planet related to fundamental upheavals, transformation and evolution, and these things can be painful, at a collective and a personal level. Pluto is named after the Greek god of the Underworld, who wore a helmet that conferred invisibility. The planet Pluto relates to things that grow silently in the darkness until they erupt, sometimes with cataclysmic results. Pluto was discovered in 1930 as the 'atomic era' was ushered in and the science of depth psychology gained ground. Its passage through Scorpio has been linked with AIDS and the growth of terrorism, among other unpleasant manifestations. However, Pluto also signifies gold and can be the source of our greatest power, which we often do not see because of our fears.

All three outer planets move slowly. Uranus takes 84 years to make a complete passage through the zodiac, Neptune 165 years and Pluto 248 years. In a natal chart they should not be interpreted personally by sign. Instead, their sign position indicates what is happening collectively, what are the general movements of which the individual is a part. Neptune especially indicates fashion and, while this may seem trivial, fashion is an indication of the underlying myth that currently inspires. For instance, Neptune was in Capricorn from 1985 until the early part of 1998, and what themes have emerged? First, everything has been 'old'. Of course, there is nothing new under the sun, but white suits, flares and platform soles certainly felt new in the late 1970s. With the passage of Neptune through Capricorn we have had 1950s revivals, 1960s revivals and, in the late 1990s, 1970s revivals. Capricorn is the sign associated with tradition and ancestry. What is in fashion is always considered glamorous, but it has been old hat, none the less. Second, there has been an emphasis on sportswear in the 1990s, especially T-shirts and trainers with the names of the manufacturers emblazoned noticeably. Sport might be better linked to a Fire sign such as Aries or Sagittarius, but we aren't really talking here about sport, we're talking about status – the kudos that comes with the inflated prices that everyone *knows* you've been able to afford, because they can see the name on your chest at 100 paces. Status is certainly a Capricornian theme. Neptune in Capricorn may also have brought an increase in cynicism and an emphasis on material gain, because Capricorn is an Earth sign that values concrete achievements and possessions. By the same token in reverse, Neptune in Capricorn may be seen as allied to the growth in Paganism – a faith that appreciates the divine within matter and honours the earth. From 1988 until January 1996 Uranus also transited Capricorn, bringing changes in business, science and government structures.

CYCLES AND CONJUNCTIONS

In addition to their movements through the signs, the outer planets (and indeed all planets, but the movements of the outer planets are more momentous) have cycles relative to each other. For example, the movement of Uranus and Neptune from one conjunction together to the next, indicates one cycle. Neptune and Uranus conjunct (i.e. come to the same place in the zodiac together) every 172 years and each time events and movements emerge that are individual to the particular age and yet part of a long-term unfoldment in human consciousness. The conjunction of these two planets in 1650 marked the execution of Charles I in England and the beginning of the age of European Classicism and Enlightenment; the 1821 conjunction saw the death of Napoleon and the acceleration of the Industrial Revolution. During these cycles events unfold and changes come about, so that the event of the conjunction is both an end and a beginning, a culmination and a denouement. The latest cycle, starting with the conjunction of Uranus and Neptune in Capricorn in 1993 has brought, for example, some changes in the ideas of the British people about their monarchy, following the divorce of the Prince and Princess of Wales. This may seem unimportant in many respects but indicates a fundamental shift in the national consciousness. The conjunction is also thought to mark the transition from industrial to post-industrial society, and to herald a new phase about which we are speculating, as these planets now take their positions in Aquarius.

Neptune and Uranus have highlighted all that is Capricornian, while also metamorphosing all that Capricorn represents, the old, the tried and tested, the traditional, the restrictive and the earth-bound. Apartheid in South Africa and the Iron Curtain have been two of the unmourned casualties. Uranus moved from Capricorn to Aquarius in 1996 and in February 1998 Neptune moved into Aquarius to join Uranus. This outer-planet movement is seen by some to be one harbinger of the Age of Aquarius. What might it mean?

INTO AQUARIUS

Capricorn is an Earth sign, representing stability, the status quo, material ambition and advancement, practicality and restraint. Aquarius, by contrast, is an Air sign of original thought, humanitarianism, innovation, independence and progress. As these planets establish themselves in Aquarius we can expect some real new vistas and it will feel as if we are in uncharted territory. Uranus is the ruler of Aquarius, so intensifying the Aquarian effect. New political ideology (with younger leaders) is likely. Greater independence for individuals and countries will be sought: the devolution of Scotland in the UK is one example of this. Laws will be questioned along with old hierarchies, such as the House of Lords in the United Kingdom. Traditional rights and customs will not be respected, but will be examined for their own merits and possibly rejected. For instance, it is unlikely that the custom of fox hunting in England will survive this Aquarian passage. Regulations regarding property are likely also to alter, with more communal ownership, idealism and sharing. Although Uranus and Neptune are both in Aquarius, as we enter the new millennium, their actual conjunction (i.e. the coming together in the same part of the heavens) occurred in the latter part of Capricorn, heralding new ideas of economics which will bear fruit in Aquarius. Companies will be run differently, with the profit ethic giving way to communal enterprise, with a greater sense of idealism and

general benefit. Thus, conservation of the environment will inevitably gain strength as an issue, and there will be a more general realisation that people have rights and that individuality is important. Companies who treat people as individuals are likely to be rewarded by a more enthusiastic workforce, ready to share ideas and feeling part of the organisation. Humanitarianism, being shown to 'pay' will be more generally adopted, resulting in accelerating reform and fresh thinking.

Computers will become ever more efficient and part of daily life in ways we are beginning to imagine, possibly more swiftly than we visualise. Children born at this time will be capable of an untrammelled vision. Held back by fewer preconceptions, they are likely to be able to follow their visions to yet more visions, expanding consciousness and making mental forays into unmapped conceptual places. Telepathy is likely to become more common. 'Anything goes' may be the motto. 'Freedom' may be another keyword as many idols bite the dust in the new century – freedom for countries, ethnic and other minorities and individuals, from anything and everything that is perceived as repressive. As elderly folk who lived through the Second World War pass on, mottos such as 'Better safe than sorry' and 'Look before you leap' will die with them, along with the remnants of the Victorian work ethic. The 'Leisure Industry' already a boom area, is likely to expand – for leisure really means time and opportunity to express yourself. As technology ever more liberates us from graft and grind and from the limitations of our own mortal inheritance, from arthritis to infertility, a new Utopia will be upon us. Would that it were that simple!

A NEW UTOPIA

A cycle is complete and Uranus and Neptune move apart in the first stage of a fresh cycle. In addition, they both leave the sign of Capricorn, tenth sign of the zodiac, to move on to its neighbour, Aquarius, the eleventh sign. Here, Neptune will remain until it establishes itself in Pisces in 2012. Uranus, moving more quickly, will stay long enough to carry us into the third millennium, finally passing into Pisces at the end of 2003. Pluto, meanwhile, is not in Aquarius, but in Sagittarius, a Fire sign, connected to philosophy and adventure. With Pluto in Sagittarius we can expect transformation of our religious institutions, our bastions of higher education and our methods of long-distance travel both mentally and physically, for these are Sagittarian motifs. In true Plutonic style, some of our over-impulsive and exaggerated enterprises may rebound to bite us on the posterior and, while we may radically transform our philosophical outlook or discover warp drive to take us to the farthest reaches of the galaxy, we may also see a rise in religious dogmatism and be confronted by some of the less desirable consequences of our tampering with nature. None the less, the passage of Pluto from Scorpio to its neighbouring Sagittarius is yet another harbinger of the millennium, drawing back the curtain on new panoramas.

There is every reason to hope and to believe that we truly are on the threshold of a new age. However, there are drawbacks to the Aquarian vision, not the least of them being the propensity to throw the baby out with the bathwater. Old institutions do have some merits, for they have withstood the test of time. Elder statesmen know a move or two not practised by whizz kids, and you can read a book by candlelight when a power cut has put your computer out of action. However, iconoclasm is the least of the Aquarian problems.

Every sign has its drawbacks. Aquarius is not better than Capricorn or its other neighbour, Pisces, which we shall be considering in the following sections. While Aquarius is humanitarian, idealistic and egalitarian, one of its chief foibles is detachment. Although the symbol for the sign is

the Water Bearer, Aquarius is an Air sign. The waters of compassion that Aquarius pours for humanity do not wet his own feet. Unlike the Water signs, who are full of feeling and who identify at an instinctual level with their fellows, with Aquarius it tends to be all ideals – the ideal of brotherhood and sisterhood, the ideal of charity, understanding, acceptance, equality, freedom. Because of this, individuals may be sacrificed, people enslaved, possessions taken away and even the right to think and feel restricted, in service to some ideal which *should* confer a better standard of living for everyone, but somehow doesn't. Terrorism, rather than dwindling before Aquarian idealism, may possibly become yet more explosive and fanatical. Aquarius is strong in the chart of communist China (charts can be drawn up for the creation of states as well as for the birth of individuals) and in that of Karl Marx. Communism is an example of something that works wonderfully in theory but in practice turns into its own opposite. And in terms of individual Aquarians, this champion of freedom may in fact be in chains imposed by their ideals, telling them they should not feel this, cannot do that. In addition, without meaning to, Aquarius may dictate to friends and family, too, for are we free to disagree on subjects such as human equality or to feel resentful or jealous when these emotions arise within us? Aquarius may not accord much freedom to human emotions or take due regard of feelings. However, only by allowing our feelings into the light of consciousness (which is different totally from acting them out) can they be transformed.

If we are to get the best from our 'Age of Aquarius' we need to be aware of the drawbacks of the sign as well as developing the fine and promising Aquarian qualities. There is much that is exciting and galvanising about Aquarius. Of all the signs, it is perhaps the most metaphorically appropriate for the huge changes and shifts of vision that appear imminent. If we can value our own frail humanity, as well as our humanitarian ideals, if we can learn to be unashamed of our darkness and if we can appreciate that the truths we perceive are our own truths, but that others may see truth from a different angle, then we will be ready for the light of the Aquarian age and be warmed rather than blinded. Utopia may take a little longer.

PRECESSION OF THE EQUINOXES

Planetary movements are part of the picture, but much longer and larger-scale movements are also operational. To understand them we need to consider certain astronomical factors. This is not always easy, for we are talking about three-dimensional events that we are *inside*, trying to understand them from our position on earth and usually having access only to two-dimensional portrayals. However, precession is essentially a simple matter and is the greatest influence considered to be connected to the Age of Aquarius.

First, let us take an outer-space perspective. Imagine the earth in space, spinning, as it does. Then imagine a giant knitting needle stuck through it. The earth spins on this needle, but the head of the needle itself also slowly describes a circle, causing the earth to 'wobble' on its axis.

Now let us move back to earth and to celestial coordinates, for we need methods of mapping our skies. This we achieve in part by conceiving great circles around us. One of these great circles is the earth's equator, projected into space. Another is the apparent path of the sun through the year, against the background of stars, called the ecliptic. The ecliptic intersects with the celestial equator twice a year, at the equinoxes, on or around 21 March and 21 September, and on these dates the sun is overhead at the equator, and day and night are of equal length all over the globe (hence

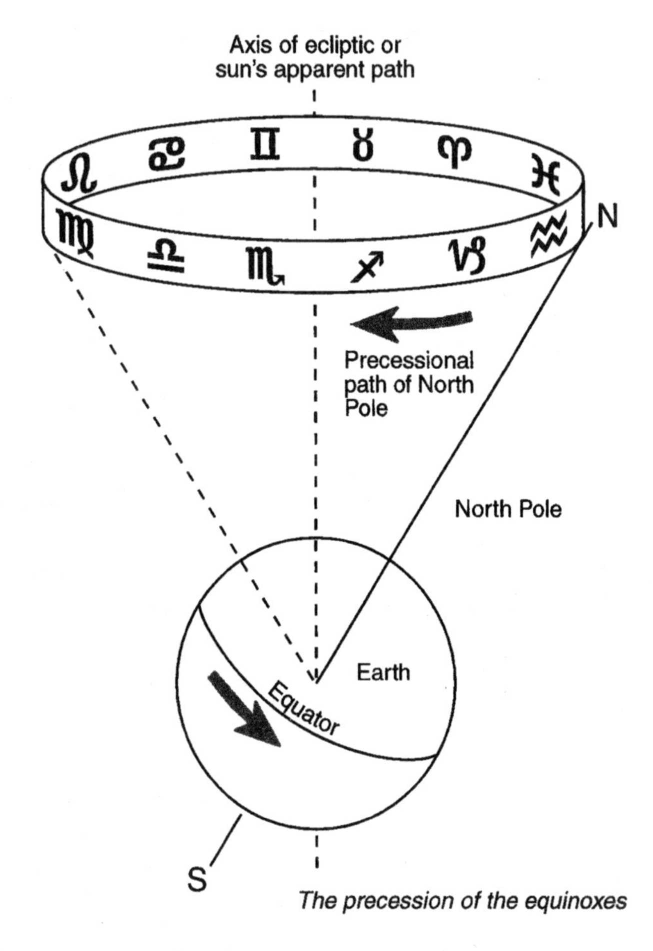

The precession of the equinoxes

the term 'equinox'). The equinox towards the end of March is called the vernal equinox because it heralds spring in the Northern Hemisphere and marks the entrance of the sun into the zodiacal sign of Aries, first of the signs, beginning the astrological year.

At the time when the signs were apparently given their names, the area of sky known as Aries did indeed coincide with the constellation, i.e. group of stars, forming Aries, the Ram. However, due to the wobble of the 'knitting needle' this is no longer the case, and the vernal point has moved backwards through the centuries, into Pisces. It is now due to move out of Pisces and into Aquarius, which means that the actual star-group the sun enters at the vernal equinox will be the sign of the Water Bearer. There is argument about exactly when this will be established, for it is hard to say exactly where one constellation ends and another begins. There are those who say this is happening now, or will happen in the early 2000s, there are others who place it further in the future, even as late as the 2800s. The complete cycle of the vernal point through all the signs takes 25,868 years, although different sources quote this figure with slight variations. This sometimes called the Great Year, Precessional Year or Platonic Year.

The phenomenon of precession has been used to castigate astrology, saying that 'the stars have moved' and so the whole thing is meaningless. Astrologers counter this by saying that astrology is based upon visible effects and that it is more likely that the signs were named after these than from imagined animals in the sky. Ordinary 'tropical' astrology is thus unashamedly based on time of year, and positions of planets relative to the ecliptic, that is on the sun's path, not on star groupings (although, of course, a picture of the starry background does vitalise astrology, emphasising our connection with the cosmos). However, there is a branch of astrology called 'sidereal' astrology, where the constellations are used, instead of the signs of the zodiac, along the ecliptic. This branch of astrology does also seem to work for certain matters and some assert that it provides better predictions. This does not invalidate astrology, by any means, but merely adds to the mystery. In interpreting the precession of the equinoxes as having meaning for the cycles of life on earth, we are, in fact, taking the perspective of sidereal astrology, or 'astrology by the stars' for we are interpreting the position of the vernal point according to the constellation inhabited.

The last 2,000 years or so have been the Age of Pisces. The birth of Christ is associated with the commencement of the Age of Pisces, and the conjunction of the planets Jupiter and Saturn in the sign of Pisces in 7 BCE probably coincided with the actual birth of Christ and was the bright 'star' that the Magi followed to his birthplace. The Three Wise Men were, in fact, astrologers, who had predicted the birth of a special person and possibly the dawning of what was at that time the new Age of Pisces. Pisces is the sign of the Fishes, and the life of Christ abounds in fish symbology such as 'fishers of men', the disciples who were fishermen, the miracle of the loaves and fishes and other factors. There is no space here to examine the full and extensive symbology of the Fish. However, the sign of Pisces represents self-sacrifice and the leaving behind of the physical world in search of the Divine. It means true identification with the suffering of others and the submergence of the paltry demands of the ego in the greater whole of the spirit. As such it represents all that is admirable in spiritual teachings.

However, abnegation of self is a tall order for most of us and there are many sides to Pisces. For one thing, there are *two* fishes and they swim in opposite directions, thus there is duality about the sign and some say that the Dark Fish leads to chaos and destruction. Pisces is also prone to deception of self and also of others. Pisces can be fearful, evasive and hypocritical. The intuitive and highly impressionable nature of the sign can be subverted to justify almost anything, including a clever and devilish cruelty, of which only those who know instinctively the vulnerable corners of the human being are actually capable. Further than this, on the zodiac wheel each sign has its opposite and it is not uncommon to find some of the worst of the polarity emerging. Opposite Pisces lies Virgo, and in the Piscean Age we have seen many picky arguments about theology, such as how many angels may fit on the top of a pinhead, and some rampant materialism which Virgo, that

Earthy sign of the practical and the particular, would be too intelligent to countenance. It is common to denigrate Pisces in favour of the clear, oncoming air of Aquarius. However, Pisces is not at fault; we have simply not risen to the occasion, so to speak. It is important that we do 'rise' to the Aquarian vibe, as the Ages change.

All the factors we mentioned as Aquarian in the preceding sections on the movements of the outer planets are operative in the Precessional Age of Aquarius, but on a grander, more long-term scale. We can expect some of the Piscean 'splits' such as matter/spirit, right/wrong and even man/woman to be transcended. The age of dualism is, in fact, on the blink as we take a wider viewpoint and see that most of our judgements are relative – heralded literally by Einstein's Theory of Relativity early in the twentieth century. Science is revealing that matter and energy are part of a continuum and that our minds influence our environment. Old dogmas are being questioned and thrown away, men and women are assuming equal status and the power of individual choice is defended. Many of these things have been developing through the twentieth century. Aquarius is the age of the Mind, when truth is sought for its own sake and no authority but that of the inner voice is heeded. There is a brilliant promise here for the progress of the human race into undreamed dimensions. But there are also drawbacks.

In considering Pisces we mentioned the Virgo polarity and how that emerged as the worst of possible Virgoan traits. Opposite Aquarius lies Leo, the Lion, and the most unpleasant of Leonine characteristics are that of egotism and power-seeking. Beneath all the detached Aquarian liberalism there may well lie an infernal powerhouse of unacknowledged oneupmanship and dogmatic adherence to one's belief, masquerading as unbiased reasoning. In addition, the Aquarian preoccupation with the cerebral could result in lives lived out in virtual reality helmets, brain

transplants undertaken without any concern for ethics, or the body wisdom that remains in muscle and gland and may fight against a new voice from the control tower, resulting in horrors that make Frankenstein look like Yogi Bear. Aquarius is a 'masculine' sign, and the equality it promises may mean that women become like men, rather than having their femininity liberated. The human consequences of lives prolonged for centuries by deep freeze, resulting in the possibility of marriage with one's own great, great grandson or daughter may not be considered by a vaunting spirit that is concerned only with what can be done, not whether it *should* be done. We have already seen the problems that can arise in this way since the atom bomb made its appearance and, unless it is addressed, the dawning of the Age of Aquarius could mean curtains for humanity. Aquarius can and should mean enlightenment for us and, if we heed its highest call to liberation, that is what it will mean, but only if we are aware enough of what and where our demons are.

PREVIOUS AGES

History gives an interesting perspective on the Precessional Ages, showing the following developments:

- **10,567 BCE Age of Leo** Hierarchies formed in society, possible formation of separate ego-consciousness in humans as opposed to the Dreamtime 'oneness', exploration. Recent discoveries suggest this may have been the time when the Sphinx was built, when 'gods' in the shape of wise and vastly superior beings walked the earth, as survivors of a cataclysm that destroyed their civilisation.
- **8411 BCE Age of Cancer** Goddess worship, matriarchal or matrifocal tribes, beginnings of agriculture and settled communities.

- **6255 BCE Age of Gemini** Invention of writing and the beginnings of dualism in conscious thought. Many migrations.
- **4099 BCE Age of Taurus** Fertility cults often centred on worship or sacrifice of bulls, such as the bull-cult in Minoan Crete and the Apis bull in Eygpt. Building of defended settlements and cities.
- **1943 BCE Age of Aries** The age of the warrior, many invasions and conquests with powerful patriarchal gods such as Yahweh and Greek Zeus. The ram god, Amon, in Eygpt and sacrifice of rams in the Old Testament.
- **213 CE Age of Pisces** Confusion, spirituality, duality, the dissolution of previous systems, which ironically have been regarded as inferior or containing 'mirages' of the superior truth now available. The symbol of Christianity is the Fish.

Naturally many elements of the above are in dispute. Also a factor that needs to be borne in mind is that here we are considering the movement of what is the vernal or spring point for the *Northern Hemisphere*. In respect of the Southern Hemisphere it may be that we should consider the opposite sign, for while the vernal point is in, say Cancer for the northern half of the globe, for the southern half it is in Capricorn. More work may need to be done on available data. However, the concept of our civilisation as part of a huge cyclical movement helps us to get our times in perspective and to realise that we are the blink of an eye in terms of great cosmic ages. This can be humbling and even frightening. Hopefully, however, it can prove a spur to considering true meanings.

ATTUNING TO THE AQUARIAN AGE

The changing times pose a challenge to each of us. Change is always frightening and we may wonder where we stand and how we will be affected by Aquarian influences. Of course, we all react differently and individually, and our own specific birth chart can reveal how the planetary movements are likely to be experienced. However, we can make some general remarks on the basis of sun sign.

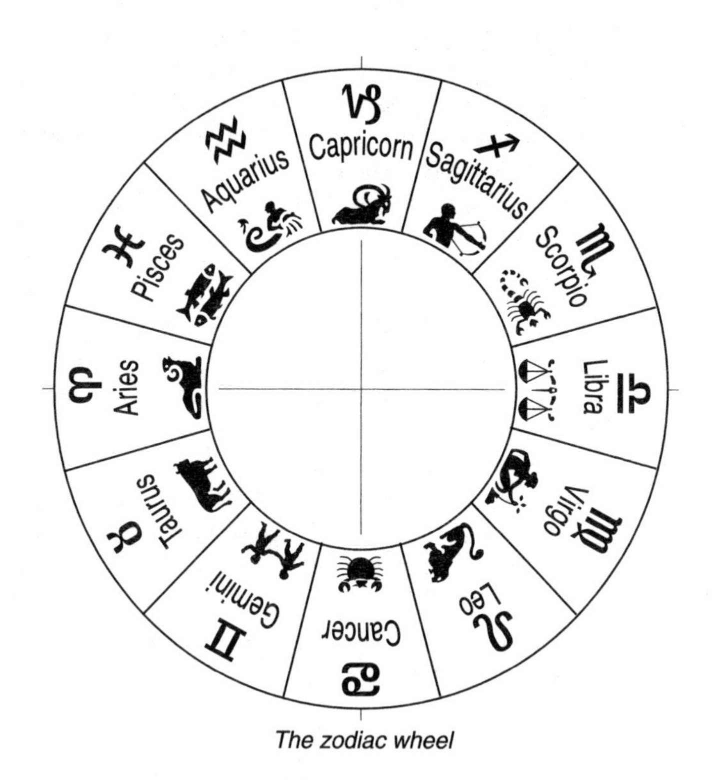

The zodiac wheel

Aries

Aries individuals, while often innovative, are likely to judge matters from a self-centred perspective. This is not intended as a criticism, for Ariens are not necessarily selfish people, out for 'the main chance' whatever the climate. However, Ariens are not likely to accept the perspectives of others, but will want to assess what the whole thing means from their point of view. If you are an Aries then you are likely to feel more at ease in the Aquarian Age, because Aquarius is really a compatible sign for you. You may feel the climate is more free, there are more opportunities and your ideas have room to grow. However, you may feel impatient with ideals that seem impractical or with 'head stuff' that never gets anywhere.

Taurus

Taurus people tend to be down to earth, valuing comfort and stability. As you rarely welcome change and feel wary of anything that threatens your nest, you may find the winds of change uncomfortable. You may fear the loss of possessions, or a threat to your way of understanding the world, and you are likely to defend what is dear to you at all costs, by digging in your heels and refusing to budge. However, many Taureans will be highly sceptical about anything 'mystical' in the first place. Some enlightened and creative Taureans are more likely to seek to 'get a handle' on what's going on and establish their corner in it. If you are a Taurus, try not to retreat into dogmatism or turn your back and pretend nothing's happening. The challenges of the new age can bring out your finest qualities of tenacity, creativity and practicality. Your influence is much needed, for you are able to flesh out the bones of idealism. Where freedom is valued you will also be free to build your castle as you see fit.

Gemini

Gemini people are usually at home with the conceptual, having quick minds and a love of new ideas and variety. Like Aquarius, yours is an Air sign, and you will find much in the new times that is in harmony with you, although you will not be quick to believe what anyone says or prophesies. Generally communicative, there may be more scope for your ideas and you may find your cerebral and quicksilver approach is increasingly valued. You may feel more free, as restraints are lifted and you are able to express yourself without excess regard for mores. As you sense opportunities you are likely to gain momentum, with idea following idea, and you will find this exciting and stimulating. However, you may become a little cynical if there is too much idealism around and you will always want to be convinced that it works. It is unlikely that you will wish to go in too deep, for you prefer to remain uncommitted and to maintain your options. There should be many choices open to you.

Cancer

Cancerians prize home, family and security. Tenacious, sensitive and intensely protective of self and loved ones, your instinct is to 'batten down the hatches' when anything threatening or even mildly unfamiliar appears on the horizon. Cancerians are more concerned with their own hearths than lighting the beacons of the New Age, and many will ignore anything significant, for as long as possible. However, many Cancerians develop a wider perspective and may become profoundly concerned with the environment and the land, which is, after all, home to us all, and will see movements afoot that they can feel enthusiastic about. When this happens Cancer places the considerable emotional force of their nature behind the matter. Aquarius is not the most compatible sign for you, but the Cancerian perspective will be deeply necessary, to keep alive the personal perspective, feelings of kinship and tradition and to prevent Aquarius throwing out the baby with the bathwater. Cancerians need to hang on to the courage of their convictions, accepting that the order must change and salvaging what is of value.

Leo

Leo is a proud sign, sunny, generous and brave, but sometimes bossy and egotistical. Leo is opposite Aquarius on the zodiac wheel, so the signs both balance each other and are sometimes at odds. You may welcome the broader perspective offered by Aquarius, the greater detachment and idealism, but you are unlikely to adjust happily in a climate where personal concerns are neglected in favour of the collective, for Leo is very much about self-expression – the great 'I am' in the nicest possible way! Leos may become champions of communal causes in ways that do feed your own egos and this is fine, but only as long as each individual Leo is aware of what is going on. It is rare for you to kid yourself that you are acting unselfishly or altruistically, because often the most delightful thing about Leo is your unashamed self-centredness. However, this charismatic sign must take care that others are not exploited and should find ways of self-expression and leadership that are responsible. Many Leos can find scope for their leadership ideas in the 'New Age'.

Virgo

Virgo people are practical, discriminating and self-possessed. You will be unconvinced about all this 'Age of Aquarius' stuff unless and until you can find reason and usefulness in it. The cerebral nature of Aquarius is to some degree compatible with Virgoan weighing of ideas and merits and you will have much to offer in terms of adding the voice of common sense. You will be able to sift the wheat from the chaff to concentrate on what is workable, not on bombast and, as always, your contribution will be invaluable. However, you are likely to become uneasy in the face of the sheer breadth of perspective that will hopefully be offered and will wish to reduce things to manageable proportions. Remember that identifying 'your' area and insisting on working within it is fine, and possibly best for you, as long as you do not forget that there are other areas, other perspectives, and use your adaptability to move from sphere to sphere, if that is indicated.

Libra

Libra is another Air sign and, as such, will find the Aquarian atmosphere congenial. You may find that your instinct for refinement and your idealism find more scope in the 'New Age' and you may feel more free to theorise and to explore new and more harmonious ways of forming relationships, where the individuality of each is honoured and the partnership is enhanced. However, you Librans are concerned about relating to other human beings and, while the theory of relationships is often your preoccupation, you hate to be alone and may find some of the more detached Aquarian vistas somewhat stark. Occasionally, Librans can be surprisingly dogmatic, so be careful you are not drawn away from true peace and beauty in this manner. You have a valuable contribution to make in softening, harmonising and adapting trends, in giving them beauty and style, both in your personal sphere and in the collective, if you so choose.

Scorpio

Scorpio, being so well-acquainted with the 'basement' of the human being, is one of the zodiac's prime cynics. It will take a lot to convince you that people are really able to change, let alone actually changing, and you will be apt to use your X-ray vision to expose the osteoporosis in new structures. Passionate, deeply sensitive and not a little secretive, you do not readily trust superficial blandishments and, because of this, you are likely to find the Aquarian climate challenging and possibly irritating. However, your approach is necessary to cut through the crap and make us all face up to what we are really feeling and what our true motives are, and so you are custodian of the dark path that is the only way to real transformation. Many individual Scorpios will concentrate on personal matters and ignore collective ones, but it is better for all concerned if you offer your two-pennyworth and put your commitment and the considerable power of your personality behind something that will make a difference.

Sagittarius

Sagittarius is the philosopher extraordinary and many Sagittarians will just love the clear breath and open vistas of Aquarius. Being for the most part cheerful, optimistic and positive, you will see much to be recommended. Some Sagittarians love playing with concepts, some with material things, like the stock market, and some of you just love to play. However, deep within the most casual and inconsequential of you there is a sage trying to get out. For all your love of freedom you are rarely an out-and-out rebel, preferring to bend the rules rather than break them, and you may even wax moralistic regarding certain extremes. Pluto will be in your sign until the year 2008 and, at some point, you are likely to experience deep personal transformation. Avoid opportunism and use your talent for finding meanings and the Divine, however you perceive it, for that will be of benefit both to you individually, and to the collective.

Capricorn

Capricorn is a practical, ambitious sign that values what is tangible and useful. Many of you will be sceptical of this 'Age of Aquarius' thing and will concentrate on the daily routine and the serious business of life. For you there is still a job to be done, even if God and all his angels are on the horizon and, in many ways, your approach is deeply stabilising and reassuring, for you deal in the manageable. Capricorn is ruled by Saturn, which was also considered to be the ruler of Aquarius until the discovery of Uranus, and the signs do share a certain sternness. You may welcome what you see as a better social order, and many Capricorns, while maintaining their feet on the ground, are attracted by the far horizons of the mystical. Having spent so much effort in getting to know this material world, Capricorn is often confronted with the inner belief that there is 'something more' although maintaining a sceptical approach. You may feel much that is irrelevant is being bandied about, but you are more capable than most of building on what is of value, personally and socially. Keep your eyes open.

Aquarius

Aquarius is the sign that may be seen as coming into its own and you may feel, or at least hope, that a more congenial order is coming where people will say what they mean, be sincere, reliable, unselfish and devoted to the common good. Indeed, this may be part of the picture, but only if some very un-Aquarian emotions, prejudices and foibles are owned and brought into the light of day, by Aquarians themselves, within themselves, as in all of us. You have the clear vision of the true idealist and you generally try to do the right thing. That is great, but please do not try to 'feel the right thing' for that will short-circuit your energies turning you into that thing you hate – the hypocrite. What you feel, however murky, is part of your humanity and we need that intact, to power the 'New Age'. Love your inner self as you love your sisters and brothers, for now we are all 'our brother's keeper'. There may be much around that you will love, but much within you will also be transmuted as Uranus and Neptune pass through your sign. Keep your feet on the ground. Do not become blinded by the light, but seek beauty in the ordinary. Rather than castles in the air seek Blake's 'Heaven in a wild flower' as a celebration of your Age.

Pisces

Pisces people are like chameleons. This sign has a reputation for mysticism, intuition and selflessness, but many Pisceans are not visibly like this at all for they take on the colour of their surroundings and may appear supremely bland or run the rat race like a hamster on a wheel. Many Pisceans will believe 'there may be something going on, but then again, perhaps not . . .' Others of you will be fascinated and deeply into crystals, dolphins and all sorts. Like Aquarius, Pisces is idealistic, but Piscean ideals are more nebulous. Some Pisceans may feel that the Aquarian promise doesn't go far enough and so may retreat, disillusioned. Others may be overcome by that tired feeling '*C'est la vie*'. Pisces is a feeling sign and no one is more able to give a human touch to the Aquarian visions than you are, for you can, at your best, both understand and see beyond. Do not be misled by the fact that we are coming out of the Age of Pisces, for this has not been an expression of the sign at its best and you may feel liberated in a fresh climate, to explore the boundless themes which are the real Piscean realm. Seek to be both kind and creative but do not sacrifice yourself, for then you have nothing left to give. Concentrate on what is being accomplished and enjoy the little things in life, as a balance.

Eclipses

Before we leave our astrological discussion of the Aquarian Age, one more factor needs to be considered. That is the eclipse of the sun that will take place on 11 August 1999.

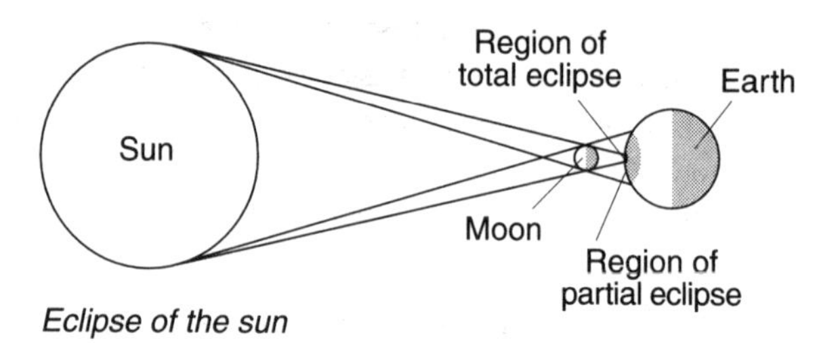

Eclipse of the sun

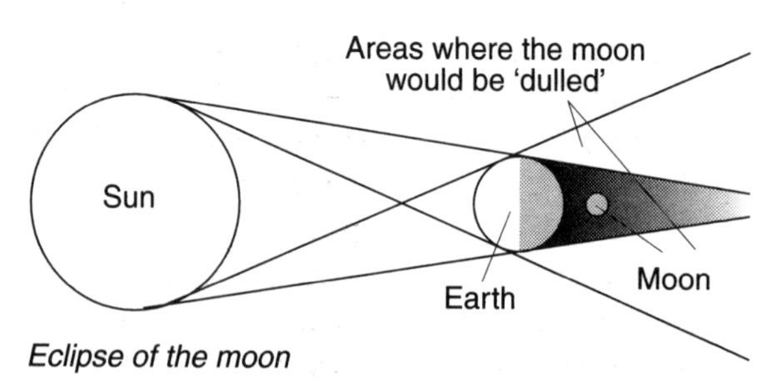

Eclipse of the moon

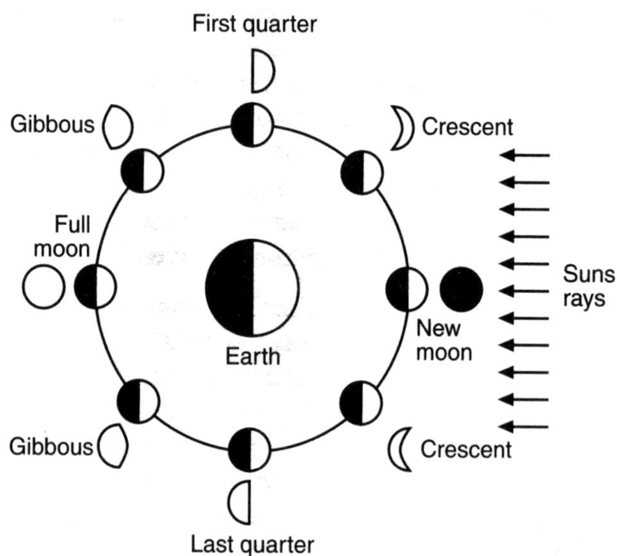

The phases of the moon as they appear in the Northern Hemisphere. In the Southern Hemisphere waxing and waning crescents are interchanged.

Birth horoscopes for ordinary individuals are a comparatively recent innovation. In classical and medieval times, the chart of the sovereign was considered the only one of any real importance, for his or her fate sealed that of the land. The cult of individualism was nonexistent and the principal job of astrology was 'mundane' which means concerned with worldly and national events. Mundane astrology is still practised today and in this branch of astrology eclipses are especially important.

There are two principal types of eclipse, that of the sun (which is eclipsed by the moon passing between sun and earth) and that of the moon (which is eclipsed by the earth coming between the sun and moon). Lunar eclipses can occur only at full moon; solar eclipses can occur only at new moon, but they do not occur at every new and full moon because the three celestial bodies have to be fairly exactly in line for the eclipse to take place. Not all eclipses are total. The moon may partly obscure the solar disc as it passes, or it may be too far from earth to cover the sun completely, resulting in an 'annular' eclipse, where a narrow ring of solar light remains, surrounding the moon. In the case of lunar eclipses, these will be total when the moon enters the umbra (see diagram) or partial or 'appulse' where the moon passes through only the penumbra. During a lunar eclipse the moon appears to turn blood red.

Astrologically, it is debatable which type of eclipse, solar or lunar, may be the most 'powerful'. In times of yore, eclipses were considered dire portents of disaster, especially to the crowned head, and the disappearance of the midday sun was particularly terrifying, earning respect and awe for the astrologers who foretold it. The eclipse takes place at the same time for the entire globe, but it will be visible only to a part of the earth's surface. As an eclipse is considered to be a special moment and a type of beginning, a 'birthchart' can be drawn up for the time of the eclipse. The signs on the eastern horizon (called the Ascendant) and on the

Midheaven will be individual for the particular place on the earth for which the chart is erected, but the planets and the eclipse itself, which is a type of conjunction (solar eclipse) or opposition (lunar eclipse) of sun and moon will, of course, be at the same point in the zodiac for all places on earth. The influence of an eclipse is said by some to extend for several days, weeks or even months on *either side* of the eclipse, for it marks part of a cycle. The chart of an eclipse can be compared with that of an individual, in some ways similar to the method we would use to compare the charts of two individuals involved in a relationship. We could gauge much of the character of the relationship from this 'synastry'. Likewise, we can obtain some idea of how an eclipse may affect an individual. If the degree of the eclipse is the same as the degree of an important planet in our chart, then we may experience either a 'wipe-out' or an intensification of that area of life.

On 1 September 1997 an eclipse of the sun took place. This was no rarity, for eclipses occur at roughly six-monthly intervals. However, it just so happened that the chart of the eclipse, drawn for Paris, showed an Ascendant of 9 degrees of Cancer, and that was exactly conjunct the natal Sun of Diana, Princess of Wales, born with the sun in 9 degrees of Cancer. Remember, an eclipse takes effect before it is exact. The day before the eclipse, Diana died in a horrific crash in a Paris underpass. Other elements in the charts, which we do not have space to examine, contain just a hint of medieval malevolence. They also suggest that in some way Diana's identity and symbolic significance blossomed due to her death, which can be seen, after all, as a type of beginning.

The 1999 eclipse

While the eclipse of September 1997 brought tragedy, both personal and national, in many respects its effects were gentle. However, the total solar eclipse scheduled for

11 August 1999 is held by some to portend something more explosive or threatening.

The chart, drawn for the eclipse, contains Sun and Moon in conjunction in the Fixed Fire sign of Leo. Mars, planet of assertion, aggression and war, forms a square or 90 degree angle to the eclipse, from the sign of Fixed Water, Scorpio. Saturn, planet of restriction and necessity, sometimes

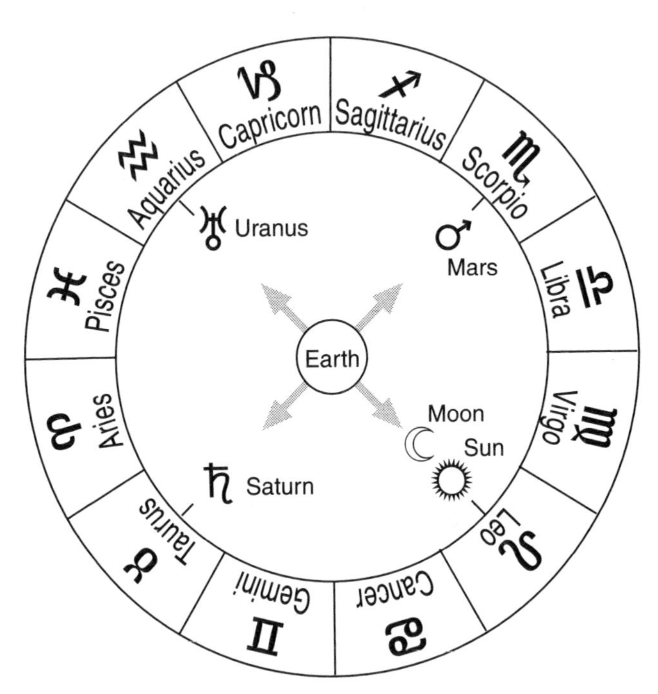

Simplified drawing of solar eclipse 11.8.99, showing only relevant planets in Grand Cross formation

equated with the 'grim reaper' also squares the eclipse, from the sign of Fixed Earth, Taurus, and Uranus, the Great Awakener, planet of rebellion, opposes the eclipse from the sign we have been talking about, Aquarius, sign of Fixed Air. Thus, what astrologers call a Grand Cross appears in the heavens and this is considered to be challenging.

In the book of Revelations in the Bible, prior to the many apocalyptic unfoldments, four beasts are described.

> *And the first beast was like a lion, and the second beast like a calf, and the third beast had a face as a man, and the fourth beast was like a flying eagle.*
>
> REVELATION 4:7

It is not hard to equate the lion with Leo or the calf with Taurus. The 'face as a man' sounds like Aquarius, which has been called the sign of Man. Scorpio, the Scorpion, appears absent at first, until one realises that the higher aspect of Scorpio is, indeed, sometimes represented as an Eagle, or a Phoenix, rising out of the flames of its own funeral pyre. Thus some people interpret this eclipse as presaging the events of Armaggedon, and great destruction as foretold in the Bible, and it is true this does look like a time of considerable stress.

However, having studied many eclipses I am more hopeful! Of course, we are well aware of the many possible disasters that as a species we are courting and there is little doubt that some of our noxious pigeons in the shape of pollution and desecration of the land are likely to come home to some unholy roosting. It would not surprise me if this eclipse equated with some disaster, natural or manmade, brought about, for instance, by unsustainable farming methods, at odds with Nature. War is also an obvious possibility, although there are wars happening all the time, in different parts of the world and we must hope that enough common sense will prevail to prevent a global conflict. None the less, in the charts of individuals, a Grand Cross, while often indicating a life of some difficulty, is often found in the nativities of highly successful people. Squares and oppositions, called 'hard' aspects, indicate challenges, not disasters, and we learn by overcoming them. Birth, for instance, is a wonderful, magical event, but the actual event of giving birth is experienced by most women as the most difficult and painful thing they have ever gone through, thus much that is highly creative involves stress and strain on the way. However, it has been said by certain writers that nations are more 'fated' than individuals, and while we may be awakened enough to make real choices in our lives, turning our difficulties into triumphs, countries tend to be more unwieldy, sliding inexorably towards whatever Fate decrees. So the eclipse could be bad news, or it could be one of the many wake-up calls we are receiving.

The eclipse of 1999 could be a difficult but rewarding birth, heralding the Aquarian Age, or it could mean some form of destruction. Perhaps it will mean both. However, the more each of us can become global citizens, forming healthy cells in the body of the collective, the more that light will spread outwards. It doesn't need all that much. One tiny virus can spawn an epidemic. By the same token, a small chink of spiritual awareness can open a pathway to the Light. The Fixed signs, Taurus, Leo, Scorpio and Aquarius do not change easily, for even while revolutionary Aquarius sometimes espouses change, they do not readily change internally. When change occurs in these signs it is often fundamental and high on the Richter scale. Astrology, while revealing patterns, also teaches us that the fault lies 'not in our stars, but in ourselves'. We do have choices, effects take place on many levels and we do create our own reality. The coming eclipse invites us to rise to the challenge and create a good one!

3

ALIEN VISITATIONS

. . . Human kind
Cannot bear very much reality.

T.S. ELIOT, *BURNT NORTON*

The idea of the 'alien' is as old as humanity. As dwarves, fairies, angels, devils, trolls, goblins and a host of other quasi-spirit beings illustrate, we seem to need a belief in 'the other'. Strange encounters are not a modern phenomenon, although they do appear to be increasing in frequency in our time. In the same way that the identity of any group is defined by the oft-persecuted outsider, perhaps we need the inhuman to confirm our humanity and to help us feel what it is to be truly human. Does this mean that such creatures are mere figments of our imagination? By no means. Is it not enormous arrogance to believe that we are the only intelligent beings in existence? As we enter the twenty-first century the meanings of aliens and the possible messages they bring is becoming the focus of much attention, for many people believe that they possess knowledge that could save or destroy us.

FLYING SAUCERS

The term 'flying saucer' came into use in 1947. Kenneth Arnold, a pilot flying for the US Forest Service in a plane especially designed for mountain rescue, was attempting to find a crashed plane when he saw nine shining saucer-shaped objects, flying between Mount Adams and Mount Rainer, in Washington State. He estimated their speed at 1,200 miles per hour. Similar objects had been seen near Ukiah on the same day. Although general ridicule made Arnold regret his disclosure, his story was followed by many others of an increasingly bizarre nature. However, these were certainly not the first strange objects to be spotted in the skies, for there had been many reported sightings in the 1890s and 1900s. Indeed, sightings of marvels in the sky go back to antiquity, and one associated idea may be that of the medieval 'fairy ship' that was said to drop anchor from the heavens. Quite aside from the unfortunately ridiculous element in the idea of a 'flying saucer' the fact is that by no means all such objects are saucer-shaped. For instance, cigar-shaped forms have been sighted, sometimes thought of as the 'mother ship' to a fleet of saucers, in addition to blobs of light that appear seemingly from nowhere and proceed to follow people around, box shapes, triangles and streaks. Shapes can change from one to another or become transparent, adding to the confusion.

Charles Fort, who has given his name to the classification of the unexplained as 'Fortean phenomena', was one of the first to go on record with ideas about the lights in the sky and their connection with extra-terrestrials. Born in 1874, Fort was a philosopher, a maverick and a journalist who loved to poke fun at the scientific establishment who, according to him, often distorted facts or were selective about them in order to advance their pet theories. Fort catalogued many scientific anomalies that are still

fascinating both to serious investigators and to those with merely a passing interest. In the case of extra-terrestrials he pointed out that such could exist, may have come before and could again, with serious consequences for all of us.

While many people simply do not want to believe in the possibility of visitors from other planets, and others have an open mind, there are also the UFO fundamentalists who believe passionately in the literal truth of extra-terrestrials and the deep significance of contact with them. Many of these are 'contactees' who believe their experience, even though it may have been little more than the sight of a glowing sphere in the sky, amounts to a spiritual revelation affecting human destiny. Face-to-face meetings with off-planet beings are not the only means of contact, for messages may also be channelled (i.e. telepathically or mediumistically received). Messages from other planets 'came through' in the table rappings of the Spiritualist Movement in the mid-1800s and channelled communications from all manner of exalted interstellar personnel are common today.

A worldwide society, named the Aetherius Society after a Venusian named Aetherius, is based on channelled communication that started in 1954 with a London taxi driver called George King, who heard voices telling him to be prepared to become the spokesperson of an interplanetary parliament. On a visit some years ago to a gathering of the Aetherius Society, what impressed me was not the fantastic nature of the information, which I am quite prepared to believe *could* be possible, but the fact that no one there seemed ever to question, suspend belief, or take into account that their perception of reality deviated hugely from the mainstream and that they could not, therefore, expect to be taken seriously by the general public, whether what they said was true or not. Because of this I could not help wondering if the believers might be on some sort of 'trip'. This is one of many factors that can make the whole UFO subject difficult to investigate.

BIGFOOT AND THE MOTHMEN

Many sightings are on record of large, hairy, humanoid creatures and these have been given a variety of names, including Yeti, Abominable Snowman and Bigfoot. Theories exist about the remnants of some 'missing link' or shy ape-like creature that still dwells in remote areas, and the continuing existence of Neanderthals has also been suggested. These furry creatures often coincide with UFO phenomena, although the manifestations are not always researched together. Bigfoot hunters are inclined to believe that this is a terrestrial creature that can be captured, although no one has yet succeeded, and hairy animals are usually ignored by the serious UFOlogist. However, the association between Bigfoot and lights in the sky endures.

A classic story on the subject concerns an Ohio family in 1981. A burnt, bare patch was found in the woods near their home, about 40 square feet in area. Ducks and chickens were found in the woods with their heads bitten off, a horse was inexplicably slashed along its side and a party of farmers, brought to haul logs, left in a hurry without offering an explanation. One night towards the end of the month of June things got much worse when a huge black 'thing' with glowing eyes appeared in the front garden. The farmer was a good shot and hit it between the eyes with his shotgun, whereupon it ran off, screaming, only to return again the next night at 2 a.m. The family got in their truck to follow it, but when they lost it they called in to enquire of a neighbour, who reported seeing nothing. Returning home they heard the sound of snapping undergrowth, and where the sounds were loudest, the truck stopped dead. Another car came on the scene and the occupants also heard growling and thrashing sounds. Managing now to start the truck, both vehicles quickly departed. However, the phenomenon of the black, hairy monsters continued to plague the family on following nights, and large footprints with three toes were found in the earth near the farmhouse, about 2 metres apart. The tracks would end suddenly and then recommence at some distance. As July progressed, lights began to be seen in the sky along with the continuing visits from the 'monsters'. Investigators arrived on the scene who corroborated the evidence from the family members. The disturbances went on for many more days, until they eventually simply tailed off, with no explanation. This is one of many stories concerning Bigfoot and, like many tales of extra-terrestrials, there is no apparent sense to it. One could be forgiven for getting the impression that something or someone only wishes to confuse and to frighten.

Many reports equally exist of hairy dwarves, but these tend to have receded in the Northern Hemisphere at least, since the 1960s, giving way to stories of the 'Greys' (see 'Abductions' below). However, there are still accounts of such creatures alive and well in South America. Sightings of winged creatures have also occurred throughout recorded history. In recent years, one such example was the 'Batman' sightings in Kent, south-east England, in the mid-1960s, but most notable in recent years were the 'Mothmen' seen in West Virginia at around the same time as other happenings such as many UFO sightings, cattle mutilations, channelled communication and technological breakdown. One notable sighting occurred on 15 November 1966, near Point Pleasant, West Virginia, where there are many abandoned buildings once used for a munitions installation. Two young couples spotted a creature, larger than a man, with great red eyes and wings folded behind it. As they drove away the thing followed them, apparently matching speeds of about 100 mph. Many other sightings took place in the same area connected with much channelled information and prophecy. One of these concerned the death of Robert Kennedy which, in fact, took place. Others predicted a huge disaster on 15 December, but this happened on 15 November, when an old bridge into Point Pleasant collapsed into the Ohio river, killing over 38 people; there were several Mothman witnesses involved in the accident.

Many strange and inexplicable creatures have been sighted, from black dogs to serpentine aquatic creatures, such as the Loch Ness Monster. While these are not necessarily connected to UFOs they all present a mystery. In times past when the eerie and unaccountable was accepted, they could have been relatively easily framed in terms of monsters, goblins, devils and hauntings, taking their place in folklore. Nowadays the only explanation that will suffice is a scientific one, and these phenomena do not appear to operate according to any known scientific laws. Should we, therefore, regard the mountain of evidence and the multitude of accounts as spurious? Or should we countenance the possibility that our current frames of reference are just too narrow?

MUTILATED ANIMALS

A sickening habit often attributed to extra-terrestrials is that of mutilating animals, mainly horses and cattle, with surgical precision and seemingly, in many cases, with great speed in broad daylight. Some nasty interference with animals has definite evidence of human involvement, such as traces of semen, and unpleasant ritual is often involved. I have often wondered if such activities are connected with the repression and exploitation of the Feminine, over many centuries. By 'the Feminine' I mean a wide sweep, including women, the Goddess and the entire natural realm of which cows with their nurturing abilities, and horses, with their curving shapes and tossing manes, are prime representatives. However, cattle and other mutilations tend to occur in greater numbers when UFO sightings are at their most frequent and most are inexplicable by ordinary means.

Attacks on herds and flocks go back into the recesses of history and were usually attributed to werewolves, vampires, trolls and the like. Corpses were often found drained of all the blood. Incidents such as this were rife along the Scottish border in 1810, in Ireland in 1874, in Guildford in 1906 and in Derbyshire in the 1920s. Today's attacks are made by a technology that experts cannot define, with precise removal of organs. In 1989 in Arkansas, five pregnant cows were found dead. Some had had parts of the rectum removed, neatly and bloodlessly, another was without an eye, another had a section of belly cut out, with the embryo, still in its sac lying on the ground nearby. In fact, there are countless reports of such happenings, from the Americas, Australia, Europe and Africa, although few from Asia. Many reports have been thoroughly verified by police and experts, with no explanation forthcoming, either for the killings and mutilations, or for the manner in which they are accomplished, which seems to be beyond our current medical abilities. Suggestions of secret experiments on the part of the government or other organisations are hardly reasonable, as these could be carried out quite easily under cover of agricultural research, or similar, giving unrestrained access to as many creatures as required. Nor does the theory of sadistic messing about or 'satanic rites' fit the facts in most cases. We are left with an alarming, distasteful and haphazard phenomenon, for which we have no satisfactory explanation at present.

ABDUCTIONS

The scariest habit of the extra-terrestrials must be that of abducting unsuspecting humans, often for tests and 'operations' and there are countless reports of such experiences. Many of these encounters involve sexual experiments and the leaving of implants in the subject that maintain contact with the aliens, but are invisible to our 'crude' technology. The beings involved have been christened the 'Greys' because of the pallor of their skin. They are reported to be small in stature, possessing psychic abilities and unimaginable scientific capabilities. Tales of aliens interbreeding with humans are not infrequent; interbreeding may be in order to improve a weakened alien stock, to strengthen the human race so it may survive a coming cataclysm, or – nastiest of all – for experimentation. One glamorous tale from 1957 tells how a 23-year-old Brazilian farmer, Antonio Villas-Boas, was abducted by aliens who stripped him and left him in the company of an unbelievably beautiful red-headed woman who seduced him with the apparent intention of impregnating herself.

Other accounts are much less pleasant and sometimes whole families are targeted for repeated abduction and experimentation. The Davis family of Indianapolis endured repeated encounters with aliens that landed in their back garden, leaving a peculiar burn mark on the ground. Family members had vague recollections of meetings with grey beings and reported blank periods in their lives. Worst of all, Kathie Davis and her husband had married earlier than planned, in 1978, because of a positive pregnancy test, only for Kathie to begin regular menstruation after an abduction experience. Hypnotherapy revealed that the father of the baby had been an alien, not her husband, and that the foetus had been removed at a time appropriate for its survival. Later she was abducted again to hold her baby, so that the aliens could study the emotional bonding and the importance of touch. This is an especially poignant account. Other tales abound, involving painful investigations, often of the rectal area or sexual organs.

Such accounts make excellent copy, for they are both sensationalist and possess some kind of hotline to a susceptible part of us connected to our nightmares, fantasies and possibly vague and repressed memories. Many such accounts are retrieved under hypnosis, and thus may be questionable in some respects for, despite the widespread use of this method and the undoubted fact that it can be useful, the unconscious mind is a mysterious territory and we cannot always be sure which 'reality' we are inhabiting. However, most contactees are not mentally ill by anyone's definition. Should we take seriously the idea of a human–alien hybrid race being formed at this crucial stage of our development? If an advanced and unscrupulous civilisation were to decide to engage in such an activity, for whatever reason, it is likely that devious and ambiguous methods would be used when going about interacting with a species as volatile and with such closed minds as ours. Or do such abductions and violations have a significance that is exclusively psychological? There is evidence to suggest that this is not 'all in the mind'.

AN ALIEN OPERATION

Not all alien interventions involve violation and experiment. Some can be benevolent and the case of Terry Walters of Berkshire, England, is an example of what appears to be a cure, effected by aliens. Terry is a successful businessman and has served as a local councillor. He certainly is 'normal' by the definition of most people. However, he has for many years been conscious of being able to hear 'voices' as if he had a radio receiver tuned inside his head. The story really begins in 1966, when Terry seriously injured his back while lifting a heavy box into the boot of his car. The damage was so bad that doctors feared he might never walk again. Painkillers were ineffective and Terry became desperate. He 'reached out' to the alien voices and begged for help.

Now began his first and quite incredible close encounter. The room was filled with light and a human-type form of pleasing appearance took his hand and he was lifted off the bed, through the closed window and along corridors into a room where he was placed on a table, on his side. The pain disappeared, leaving only numbness. The alien looked at him hypnotically and he became aware that other aliens were working on his back, painlessly. When he caught a glimpse of them they appeared different from his rescuer, smaller and reptilian. Terry described himself as 'terrified' even though he was aware that the aliens were benevolent. Suddenly he found himself back on his bed, sitting upright, with sweat dripping off him. His impulse was to call his wife and tell her what had happened, but something stopped him and he spoke only of an 'amazing experience'. All that was left was a numbness in his back and the next day he went to work as usual.

Life proceeded as usual and Terry enjoyed business success. In 1985 his back troubled him once more and he was sent for an X-ray in Heatherwood Hospital in Ascot, Berkshire. He was also given blood and tissue tests. When he came back for the results, two weeks later, he was faced by a panel of 18 medical specialists who questioned him in depth about his diet, whether his work involved unusual substances, and where he had had the operation on his back that did not appear on his medical records! He insisted he had not undergone surgery, but the X-rays revealed evidence of an operation quite beyond the capabilities of modern technology. In addition, his blood contained seven unidentifiable substances, as well as giving figures which should have meant that he was currently dying of rare skin cancer! More tests have since shown that the highly sophisticated operation was a reality. Terry Walters should be a cripple, at best. However, he is well and active, his work involving much physical activity.

Terry is intrigued by what has happened to him and has spent considerable sums of his own money on the investigation of his operation. There is no explanation of what happened to him that fits in with current scientific belief. Indeed, the above account reads like rather far-fetched sci-fi, yet several elements in it have been verified. However, Terry's experience serves as an example of a positive encounter, with what were, apparently, helpful aliens who healed him. (A fuller account of these events can be found in *Quest* magazine, Issue 6, April/May 1996. See Further Reading.)

CONSPIRACY THEORIES

In a world of exploitation, deception, cynicism, power games and corruption, it is no wonder that we may suspect governments and large organisations of 'cover-ups'. It is well known that countries have a Secret Service and that this may be used to infiltrate and influence the affairs of enemies and neighbours, and there are plenty of documented cases where governments have unsuccessfully tried to cover up the truth. How many times are such cover-ups successful? Nazi Germany, with some justification, is believed to have employed occult forces as part of its strategy of conquest. Some people believe that this went further and that the Nazis possessed an advanced 'occult' technology that produced shape-shifting flying machines, and that related research is conducted at secret military installations to this day.

Perhaps the most famous of all 'flying saucer' incidents was that which took place at Roswell in the American Southwest in 1947. Newspaper reports described 'a flying disc of unknown origin' found by airforce personnel, including a curious foil-like substance with strange properties. Suddenly all communication was forbidden by the military and the affair was declared a terrible mistake, the unidentified object having been a crashed air balloon, all along. However, the story did not go away and rumours persisted, including that of retrieved alien corpses upon which autopsies had been performed. Witnesses were mysteriously silenced and a nurse who said she had taken part in the post-mortems died in a plane crash. More than 300 witnesses were found of this incident and 50 of them said they knew alien bodies were retrieved by the military. The Roswell incident has become a UFO classic.

Another crash of presumed extra-terrestrial craft occurred in New Mexico in 1948. This object had reportedly been located on radar which had disrupted its controls. Grey alien bodies of small stature were recovered and the object was taken to Wright-Patterson Air Force Base. There have been many reports of similar incidents, mostly less dramatic, over the last 50 years, leading to a belief in some quarters that we are regularly being visited by extra-terrestrials, in league with governments, who are being allowed to take people for 'experimentation' in exchange for alien technology. An investigation was started in March 1952, by the US Air Force, to look into the existence of flying saucers. After extensive interviews with contactees and other research, this operation, known as Project Blue Book, concluded in December 1969 that there was no evidence to support the existence of alien craft. However, many of the associated documents are still classified and this operation did nothing to enhance public trust of the US government regarding the entire subject.

In 1982 a mysterious package arrived for a UFO researcher called Bill Murray. This contained a film of a document concerning 'Operation Majestic' for President Eisenhower, a highly classified piece of information. This stated that four extra-terrestrial bodies had been recovered at Roswell and that information had been covered up for reasons of national security. Twelve senior personnel drawn from the military and scientific communities were named and an FBI investigation was instituted into the entire affair. The possibility of fraud on the part of Bill Murray and Jamie Shandera, a television producer also involved, was considered, along with disinformation and cover-up. A dead end was reached, with many Air Force officers retiring to claim immunity from questioning as private citizens. The final conclusion suggested that the group of investigators looking into the matter were themselves possible fabricators of Operation Majestic. Good *X Files* material! Other military personnel have gone on record regarding government treaties with aliens. These include Major Donald Keyhoe, who released articles and books in 1950 stating that earth was under surveillance by extra-terrestrials and that this was well known to the air force command personnel. Another is former Naval Officer Bill Cooper, who stated that aliens were conducting experiments on cattle and humans and the government was frightened by their lack of control of them. Many rumours also abound concerning 'Area 51' at Groom Lake in Nevada, where many mysterious experiments are said to take place, in addition to development of Stealth, SDI and other highly classified projects. Area 51 has become the centre of suspicion for those who believe in alien conspiracies.

So what may be the truth of the matter? One thing seems certain to me. If there is a conspiracy it can surely not involve too many people or there would be many leaks – more even than suggested by reports. In addition, what could be more useful as a cover-up for some real controversial weapons and similar research than the skilful generation of UFO incidents, to distract the public? Belief in conspiracy is seductive and insidious, for it enables us to project our fears and definitions of evil outside ourselves and names a convenient enemy. Having said this, it can surely not be regarded as impossible that certain people have dealings with alien life-forms for whatever reason and this would, in all probability, be conducted away from the public gaze, in order not to cause panic, witch hunts or similar extreme reaction.

TWISTS IN TIME

One of the stories that has prime place in UFO folklore is that of the Philadelphia Experiment. Dr Morris K. Jessup, in the 1950s, researched a story about experiments on invisibility by the United States military, conducted during the Second World War. In October 1943 the Navy induced a tremendously powerful magnetic field on a destroyer on the Delaware River in Philadelphia, with the result that the ship disappeared and reappeared in Newport, Virginia. The sailors became almost transparent to each other. Some went into a kind of 'deep freeze' and had to be treated by other electronic equipment to thaw out. One man disappeared in full view of his wife and children, two others burst into flame and burnt for 18 days. There are other versions of this strange tale that come from behind what used to be the Iron Curtain, alleging that the Americans were experimenting with strong magnetic fields in the shape of a Moebius Strip. Three UFOs were spotted in the area in the days prior to the experiment and it is believed that a UFO was 'caught' in this process, flying over the ill-fated ship (or, some say, submarine) as it disappeared.

Connected to this are more recent accounts of the Montauk Project, recounted in the book *The Montauk Project* by Preston Nichols in 1993, where he states the Philadelphia Experiment was ostensibly closed but research continued secretly at New York's Montauk Air Force Base. Here

attempts were made, or are being made, to travel in time and manipulate its flow. The account of this, given in *Alien Impact* by Michael Craft, includes stories that are difficult for even the most open-minded of us to entertain. UFO conspiracy, pyramids on Mars, time travel, people brainwashed into travelling to other dimensions through reprogramming techniques borrowed from tantric sexuality, travellers lost in other dimensions, psychic powers exploited by technology and many others, including encounter with Jesus Christ on Mars! People involved in these experiments have usually been hypnotised or 'reprogramed' into forgetting their experiences. However, in some cases they have resurfaced at a later time. One central idea is that the aliens from the UFO 'caught' in the Philadelphia Experiment are involved with these matters. In addition, certain persons from the Philadelphia incident 'fell through time' into 1983 and had to be sent back, using alien technology, to prevent the expansion of a hyperspace bubble caused by the ill-fated experiment.

From the point of view of the new millennium, the punchline concerns the 'end of time' in 2012, due to a loop caused by what happened in Philadelphia. Travellers beyond this point find that everything goes hazy and there are no people to be seen, but 'a different kind of reality'. As most of these stories sound too far-fetched even for a good sci-fi movie, one might be justified in asking 'So what?'. However, the date of 2012 ties in uncannily with Mayan and Hopi prophecies – which may, of course, have been familiar to those who 'remember' being involved in the Montauk Project. Another explanation is that these time experiments are being undertaken under the auspices of the Greys and that they are linked to other experiments of the same type. The last one of these will be in 2012, and that is why a 'wall' is encountered beyond this year. One of the challenges of the new millennium may be a change in consciousness and the beginnings of comprehension of other dimensions. Is this all rubbish, or is truth here really stranger than fiction? Maybe we do not know as much about 'reality' as we believe.

FAIRIES?

There is a wealth of folklore on the subject of 'the little people' – fairies, goblins, elves, leprechauns. These have been with us for centuries. Children are raised on fairy stories and fairies are part of the subconscious dreamworld of most of us, although their reality is generally scoffed at. Are all fairy stories simply a product of the superstition of primitive folk, or do they bear some relation to fact?

The term 'nature spirits' is generally more acceptable and it was to these beings that the Findhorn Community, in Scotland, attributed their success in raising plants in a cold and inclement area. By specifically seeking to make contact and co-operate with these beings, spectacular results were obtained, growing 18 kg (40 lb) cabbages and foxgloves well over 2 metres (6 feet) tall. One of the community even persuaded the moles to leave the garden alone by visualising an audience with 'King Mole' which resulted in the moles withdrawing to adjacent scrubland. This encounter could perhaps more aptly be described as a 'shamanic journey' or experience of spirit flight – a practice common in most ancient cultures. Whether the 'King Mole' was 'real' or not did not make any difference to the result. The Findhorn Community identified several forms of nature spirits, from the devas who are species archetypes, to elementals who care for plants, minerals and water supply. We may greet this with scepticism, but basically what the Findhorn Community did was to treat the earth, plants, streams and such like as if they were sentient and with respect. By doing this they achieved monumental results.

Traditional encounters with 'fairies' have not generally proved so bountiful, for fairies have been known to be tricky things. One of their habits is/was that of abducting human children, particularly those who were especially beautiful and placing in their stead a fairy creature who resembled the child, through 'glamour' but might in reality have been a wizened and twisted goblin. Fairies also were known to abduct people. People who entered the fairy kingdom lost all sense of time and one night in fairyland could mean that one re-entered the everyday world to find a century had passed and everything one had once known had passed away. One of the most famous fairy 'abductees' was Thomas the Rhymer, also known as Thomas of Ercledoune, who lived in the thirteenth century. He was taken to the traditional haunt of the Queen of Elfland, beneath the barrow-mounds, and from his experience there he was enabled to make many prophecies. While many of his predictions came true, his forecast of a huge natural disaster in the nineteenth century did not, despite the fact that thousands of English peasants fled to high ground for safety.

Descriptions of some fairies match those of the Greys, the aliens who are reputed to abduct people for experiments. Fairies were also said to drain blood from cattle and to display many of the characteristics associated with aliens. The fairy habit of abducting humans is reminiscent of alien practice. It is interesting that UFO activity has been associated with certain ancient structures, such as barrow-mounds, which are also the reputed haunt of the people of Otherworld. Could it be that aliens have been with us for centuries and we are only now coming to realise that they are, for the most part, extra-terrestrials? Or perhaps the concept of extra-terrestrials is simply more acceptable to the 'space age' mind set.

CROP CIRCLES

Crop circles have become a prevalent modern phenomenon, where stalks in fields of grass or grain are flattened, but not broken, in a regular design, usually circular. These tend to occur where UFOs and other unexplained phenomena are more prevalent. Although widely believed to be a modern phenomenon, there have been documented cases since medieval times, which hardly lends support to the belief that such circles are hoaxes. Crop circles are especially common in the southern counties of England, although they appear all over the world. Edwin Fuhr, a Canadian farmer, may have been one of the few people to observe a circle being formed when, in 1974, he noticed five shiny round objects floating a foot off the ground over his rape field, emitting a vapour that pushed down the stalks. During the 1990s the shapes became more and more complex, appearing in geometric shapes such as a 'Mandelbrot set', serpents, dolphins, flowers and even a message in a strange, rune-like script called Senzar that was deciphered as spelling out the name of the Egyptian god of the primeval waters and regenerative force, Ptah.

Many theories have been postulated about these circles. Since J.E. Lovelock formulated the 'Gaia' hypothesis the notion has been entertained that earth is a sentient, self-regulating organism, upon whom life did not arise and does not continue through the laws of chance but through a controlling and balancing agency, namely the earth itself. Indigenous peoples have described crop circles as 'the earth screaming'. The writer David Elkington likens them to a rash: 'What happens to a person if they cannot speak, if they are frustrated, ignored, shouted down? In all probability they come out in a nervous rash.' We 'shout down' the voice of nature, metaphorically, with our technology and literally as electromagnetic vibration distorts the natural emanations of the earth. The crop circle competition held on 11–12 July in

Buckinghamshire proved that many designs could be fakes and provided opportunity for sceptics to cease to treat the entire matter in any way seriously. However, hoaxes cannot account for all the circles, unless there is a worldwide conspiracy to provide designs large and small, of great intricacy or extreme simplicity – and unless there were hoaxers out to bemuse medieval peasants also.

In contrast to our sad habit of exploitation, certain native peoples have maintained their tradition of living in harmony with the earth. Among the most notable of these are the Hopi Indians. Their prophecies, which predict the coming destruction of the world as we know it, are encoded in figures engraved on the side of cliffs in the Hopi territory. (We discuss this in more detail in Chapter 4.) These petroglyphs are similar in design to many of the crop circles found in Britain, and have been interpreted by Hopi elders as indicating that an ending is imminent. Is someone or something trying to tell us something? We feel much more comfortable believing in hoaxes!

SEEDLINGS OF THE STARS?

There have been many speculations regarding the genesis of civilisation and even our species itself, through the agency of extra-terrestrial beings. There are many factors to suggest this. For instance, how did ancient peoples, living according to our knowledge of history, in a crude and primitive manner, manage to move and chisel to paper-thin accuracy huge blocks of stone many tonnes in weight? Buildings involving these stones are found as far apart as Egypt and South America, and we have no way of constructing them today. And how is it that a highly sophisticated knowledge of astronomy was also possessed, millennia ago, by the same people who moved the enormous stones? The astronomical sophistication of such structures as Stonehenge and the pyramids is only just becoming apparent as our knowledge catches up! Another oft-quoted fact is that the Dogon tribe, from Africa, have always known that Sirius was a double star, a binary system of a visible star and a white dwarf of enormous density known as Sirius B. The Dogon believe all creation came from Sirius B. They know that it is small and heavy and that it travels around Sirius A in an ellipse, with an orbital period of 50 years. Could this have been because their tradition has been passed down the generations from the time the partner to Sirius was still visible, or did they receive this knowledge from Sirian visitors? Also, why do so many languages, from opposite sides of the globe, possess a common source? Discovery of old maps of a standard suggesting aerial flight such as the Piri Re'is map, belonging to a Turkish pirate in the sixteenth century, and apparent 'landing strips' located in the Nazca pampas in Meso-America have added fuel to speculations that visitors from outer space landed on earth in prehistoric times and laid a guiding hand upon our primitive forebears.

These theories became popular in the 1960s and 1970s, due to the books by Erich von Daniken, *Chariots of the Gods?* and *Gold of the Gods*. Von Daniken's work has since been discredited as of poor scholarship, wildly speculative and, at times, lacking common sense. Academics refuse to take such ideas seriously, referring to them in rather emotive terms as 'preposterous'. This is a shame, because it prevents the theory achieving a sensible airing. Of course, there are other explanations for many of these mysteries, and one that tends to be espoused by writers such as Robert Bauval, Colin Wilson, Graham Hancock and Maurice Cotterell is that humanity and civilisation are actually far, far older than we have believed and that previous civilisations may have been much more advanced. Lines on the Nazca pampas are also attributable to a culture that practised spirit flight and the idea of straightness connected to shamanic

journeys. None the less, however strange it must doubtless seem to our earthbound selves and, however insulting to our egos, it is surely not impossible that, at some point in time, highly advanced extra-terrestrials did land in our world and manipulate it.

Our received wisdom is full of OOPARTs, a term coined by the naturalist Ivan Sanderson, for out-of-place artefacts. These include articles of machined iron found beneath tons of unquarried coal, optical lenses many thousands of years old and ancient maps, such as the aforementioned Piri Re'is map, showing Antarctica without the ice caps. One immense OOPART is that of the Sumerian civilisation, that appeared apparently out of nowhere. In *Alien Impact*, Michael Craft makes the point: 'This civilisation did not slowly develop; it was "instantly" there, writing, buildings, art, everything. This mystery is the real foundation of the Ancient Astronaut Theory.'

Michael Craft also makes the valid point that we take ancient texts at face value when they involve wars, shipping and trade, but when in almost the same breath the 'gods' are referred to, we assume this is a fanciful aberration of a primitive imagination. But what if they were telling the literal truth and the 'gods' really did exist as physical beings in the same time and space (i.e. powerful visitors from outer space)? Sumerian writings, such as the *Enuma Elish* can be interpreted as the activities of mighty beings from other planets. The writer, Zacariah Sitchin, an ancient astronaut theorist, has another interpretation of the Sumerian myth of the slaying of the dragon Tiamat by her great-great-great grandson, Marduk. Legend tells that this primordial dragon gave her body to make the world and many have seen her murder by Marduk as a metaphor for patriarchal takeover of the powers of the great Mother Goddess. However, drawing upon Sumerian texts, Sitchin believes that Marduk was, and is, a huge maverick planet orbiting the sun in a great ellipse and having its own internal heat source.

Marduk smashed into the planet Tiamat and it split into the asteroid belt and a fiery ball of rock that was pulled in closer to the sun and subsequently cooled, to form our earth. It was seeded with genetic material from the destructor, Marduk. Such an interpretation of Sumerian myth encompasses billions of years, from the creation of our planet, to the growth of life on Marduk and its transfer to earth. Later on in time, for purposes of their own technology and survival, the inhabitants of Marduk, the Anunnaki (also called the Nefilim) came to earth and interbred with the primitive humanoids. The Nefilim appear again in Chapter 7. These 'gods' retreated to safety when the approach of Marduk caused the melting of the polar ice caps, resulting in the Great Flood. This flood is part of the mythic inheritance of most countries. The biblical survivor is called Noah, the Sumerian survivor is called Utnapishtim. Both of these were warned by the 'gods' to build a craft that would survive the deluge. These gods used humanity as chess pieces in their wars with each other, resulting in nuclear explosions in prehistory, destroying Sodom and Gommorah and causing the contamination of springs around the dead sea with dangerous amounts of radioactivity.

Many elements in modern astronomical knowledge support the theory of the existence of a planet such as Marduk, and there has indeed been evidence supplied by the orbiting telescope IRAS of a large body, the size of Jupiter, sited out towards Orion but close enough to be part of our solar system, and this large body is coming nearer to earth. Other relevant facts include the erratic orbit of Pluto and its size, which is small for an object so far from the sun – in fact, Pluto is only two-thirds the size of our own moon. A likely explanation is that it was a moon of one of the outer planets, pulled out of orbit by a huge gravitational field. The asteroid belt has been believed to be the remains of a destroyed planet, but there is not enough mass in the combined asteroids to account for this – unless one includes the mass of the planet earth in the calculations. Also there is a huge gash in the surface of Miranda, one of the moons of Uranus, that looks as if it were made by something unbelievably enormous. Many historians believe that earth has been visited by several catastrophes in history that account for sudden extinction of species and many geographic anomalies. In additional support of the theory, Sumerian astronomy has proved highly accurate, down to a description of the appearance of Neptune confirmed by *Voyager 2* and disaster happening to Uranus, which knocked it on to its side. This the Sumerians attributed to collision with Marduk. The Sumerians also believed in a tenth planet (i.e. Marduk), for which astronomers are still searching. Perhaps we had better hurry up; Marduk and the old gods may be on their way towards us.

TOWARDS A NEW 'REALITY'

In this chapter we have ranged through a wide variety of extremely far-fetched anecdotes and beliefs. Are we to regard all of this as complete rubbish, fantastical and insane concoctions, or might there be some sort of message here for us that we are being challenged to decode, as the twenty-first century opens? The old saying 'There's no smoke without fire' springs to mind. And yet what are we to make of nonsensical practices such as keyhole surgery on cattle and Bigfoots that appear and disappear with the apparent intent only of frightening and confusing us? Like so much in the way of 'psychic phenomena' there is enough evidence to convince those who wish to be convinced and not enough to be accepted as proof by the sceptic.

The pioneering psychologist and erstwhile disciple of Freud, C.G. Jung postulated the existence of a 'collective unconscious' shared by the whole of humanity. Within this collective certain symbols have universal meaning and one of the most powerful of these is the circle, or circular pattern, called a mandala and signifying balance and completeness in the personality. One suggestion concerning flying saucers is that they are images arising spontaneously in the collective unconscious, mandala shapes calling us to awaken to a new consciousness, a new wholeness. This may be seen as a reductive approach, where all manifestations are attributed to the human mind, and yet this approach at least brings us to ask why we are seeing these objects, in this way, at this point in our history.

Shamanism has been called the 'oldest spiritual discipline' on earth and many cultures have a shamanic thread, running from prehistoric times. The shaman was a respected figure in the community, undertaking gruelling 'spirit flights' in order to pick up information from the 'gods' or spirits that were of assistance to the tribe. In Jungian parlance, one might perhaps say the shaman's journey actually takes place in the realm of the collective unconscious. This process is currently being revived in shamanic lodges and groups, where individuals seek to retrieve the wisdom teachings of the Native Americans and other indigenous peoples. Shamanism is a process of directed trance for, unlike a medium, the shaman is not 'taken over'. The elements of the shamanic journey, which always has a purpose, are recalled and interpreted by modern practitioners. While there are those who journey to effect healing and for similar purposes, many people simply take part in order to achieve personal revelation, to 'find themselves'. Many beings may be encountered upon these out-of-body travels. Among the more seasoned Native American practitioners, meetings with extra-terrestrials have taken place, such as the vision of an awesome being who will come and switch off all civilisation's generated power, from electric lights to nuclear weapons before the end of the twentieth century, experienced by the seer and healer John Lame Deer.

It is the function of the shaman, in a sense, to break through the bounds of 'ordinary' reality to access knowledge from another dimension, another state of consciousness. In the civilised world we have no place for such activity and we regard those who have vivid experiences that could be termed 'shamanic' as peculiar, or mad. We make little effort to adjust our viewpoint on the basis of occurrences that do not fit in with our current paradigms. We assume there must be another explanation, that there is a hoaxer at work or that those who see aliens and such like are deceiving themselves. But what if we are deceived?

Suppose that we were to return to medieval Europe, in a time machine. We would have to be very careful. Any suggestion of the technology we take for granted would get us, in all probability, into a great deal of trouble. The possession of something as simple as a battery torch might get us burnt at the stake as a practitioner of the black arts. Have we really changed that much? In some ways and in some places there are, indeed, more freedoms, tolerance and open-mindedness, but in many others the old attitudes prevail in one guise or another. And it is doubtful whether even the most tolerant and futuristic of us would regard an influx of extra-terrestrials as anything but threatening – possibly with good reason. Therefore, surely any sensible visitors from outer space would come heavily disguised, for their own protection, appearing only to a select few, or in cases where circumstances required them to reveal themselves. If 'they' are here, we are unlikely to know about it, until 'they' wish us to.

In a world denuded of spirituality, science has become our god and we forget that science is a way of talking about reality, a creation of working models. What we see, hear, taste and touch, and what science tells us is *not* reality, or at least not the entire picture. The closest we may come to a comprehension of reality is that the universe is a vibration.

Light is a vibration, turned by our eyes and brains into colours and shapes; sound is a vibration, heard by our ears as the discordant or the musical; our bodies are vibrations, millions of particles of energy vibrating at a certain rate. Science has informed us of this, but it cannot give us a perception of it, nor can it make total sense of the picture as the 'smallest' particles break down into smaller, and yet smaller particles, suggesting an infinity of – what? The essence slips away from under the microscope. Of course, this is not an invitation to believe anything and everything, like credulous fools, but it does ask for a mind open to the unthinkable.

Is it not possible that we are, as many writers, seers and prophets have suggested, on the brink of a new consciousness? Are we ready to make some breakthrough in our evolution, into a fresh comprehension of the universe? It is hard to imagine the existence of other dimensions, and we can readily do this only by analogy. Imagine a two-dimensional world of Flatland, where the inhabitants were aware only of length and breadth; for them height had no existence. And then imagine a three-dimensional being like ourselves interacting with them and attempting to communicate. This would be extremely difficult, for we would have no frames of reference for our three-dimensional consciousness in their terminology. Our manifestations would seem miraculous and probably haphazard and most mysterious – just like the 'alien' phenomena we have been discussing. Communicating with them and making them aware of our world would be difficult and frustrating in the extreme. And now suppose that some of our 'aliens' are, in fact, consciousnesses from a further dimension. Would not this go some way towards explaining the sheer 'oddness' of their activities?

Perhaps we are being reconditioned, in order to break down our limited world view. In *Alien Impact*, Michael Craft quotes researcher Jacques Vallee as saying 'If the

phenomenon is forcing us through a learning curve IT HAS NO CHOICE BUT TO MISLEAD US'. Craft goes on to say, 'Like rats in a maze we are being conditioned by a phenomenon that occurs in regular cycles, yet remains unpredictable. If the stimulus is unpleasant, the rat is under pressure to engage in new behaviour.' What is that new behaviour? Whether we are being 'reconditioned' by actual beings from other planets or dimensions or by our own inner or higher selves, it is hard to envisage what the next step in our evolution may be because, in a sense, if we can imagine it then we have already taken that step. Perhaps the new consciousness may encompass a different view of time, which may be the next dimension through which we currently move, without control of our destiny. Part of the 'new consciousness' may be a global or indeed universal 'knowingness' that extends beyond our personal confines – a knowledge of our past, our future and our destiny and purpose. Whatever the case, in this direction surely lies the way for us to stop our self-destructive behaviour and 'man's inhumanity to man' and to the ecosystem. We do not have to 'believe' all the phenomena, but perhaps we do have to 'open' to them in some way. Here may lie a way forward.

4

PROPHECIES

. . . I did know that the purpose of a prophet was to be wrong, that what a prophet does is give a wake-up call. If the prophet is successful we hear the call and the prophecy does not come true.

BOB FRISSELL

Many prophecies cluster around the turn of the millennium and the early years of the twenty-first century. Some say that invaders from outer space will arrive and take over our world. In some accounts these invaders are benevolent, in others they are less so. Some predict a huge battle in which billions of souls will perish. Others foresee natural disasters such as the most enormous earthquake in history, collision with a large comet or meteor, or a shift of the poles. Less extreme disasters include those brought about by pollution, deforestation, the greenhouse effect, the depleted ozone layer and the advent of a 'super-bug' produced through over-use of antibiotics or unnatural farming methods, causing an epidemic that kills large numbers of people.

Cheerful predictions are less sensational, but they do exist, suggesting an opportunity for world peace and a rise in the

level of collective consciousness, which can be defined in several ways. I believe our general sense of guilt disposes us to harp on about the unpleasant prophecies. That guilt probably arises from our estrangement from our own essential selves and from our connection with the cosmos that we noted in Chapter 1 – our 'original sin' of becoming stranded in our detached minds, apart from the mainstream of creation and instinctual participation in life. Lots of people fear they are 'bad' but it is not what they have done, or anyone else did in the past but what most of us are no longer able to do that is the problem. That is, we rarely feel we are a vibrant part of a great and inspiring picture, we do not have the 'peak' experiences of mystical oneness and joy that we 'should' have, and so we feel 'wrong'. But perhaps we are on a journey.

Several of the more disturbing predictions have not materialised on time.

- **1914** This was predicted as the Year of Armageddon by Jehovah's Witnesses. This date was compiled from the Bible (Daniel 4), where 'seven times' are mentioned. A 'time' was taken as being 360 days, making 2,520 days in total. Using the 'year for a day' conversion, also from the Bible, this was estimated to be 2,520 years which, measured from 607 BCE, indicated 1914. Of course, as we know, the First World War did break out in that year, but the world did not end.
- **1957** A Californian pastor foretold that 'Sometime between April 16 and 23, 1957, Armageddon will sweep the world. Millions of persons will perish in its flames and the land will be scorched.'
- **1984–1999** Bhagwan Shree Rajneesh, Guru of the Rajneesh movement, predicted many massive disasters on earth, both natural and manmade. Floods, earthquakes, volcanic eruptions and nuclear wars. New

York, San Francisco, Los Angeles, Bombay and Tokyo will all disappear.

- **1995** David Koresh of the Branch Dividian Group in Waco, Texas, computed the imminent end of the world, from texts in the Bible. On 10 April 1993, 76 commune members died as a result of fire, started deliberately.
- **1996** A book *The Return of Jupiter: End of the World in the light of the Bible* issued by Dorrance Publishing, Pittsburgh PA, predicted disaster starting beneath the Pacific, when a terrible earthquake was expected to break the crust of the earth.
- **1996, 23 October** James Ussher, an Irish Archbishop of the seventeenth century, estimated that the first day of creation took place on 23 October 4004 BCE, 4,000 years before the commonly accepted true birthdate of Christ, and that the end of the world would occur exactly 6,000 years later.
- **1998, sometime** An active religious organisation called 'Centro' centred principally in the Philippines, predicted the end of the world in 1998.

The end of the world was also fully expected in the year 1,000 and there occurred much civil unrest as that time came close. When nothing happened the Church was criticised, resulting in a backlash in which heretics were exterminated wholesale. It seems impossible that such events could be repeated precisely. However, the millennium is sure to cause stress and upheaval in the mass psyche and many irrational and unexpected things may happen before we all settle down again.

HOPI INDIAN PROPHECY

The Hopi Indians live in close identification with their mythology maintaining their sacred trust with the land,

living peacefully and with a quiet pride. Their home is in north Arizona, the sacred mountain of Black Mesa that rises from the desert and is regarded as an important 'energy centre' upon the earth and the spiritual nexus of the continent. Hopi life is simple and very hard. Tilling the land and carrying water are interspersed with prayer and the Hopi have learnt to from a harmonious relationship with the harsh country that is their home. To the Hopi all things are alive and sacred, and they live in close communion with the Earth Mother.

It is the Hopi myth that vitalises and gives meaning to their life – and in this sense 'myth' means important allegory, inspiring story, not fiction. In this myth the story of creation is told, from the beginning of the Hopi nation to the time when the Great Spirit will return, with the Great Purification. The tale unfolds as follows:

At the time when the third world was destroyed through a shift in the poles (the third world was the one before our present one), some individuals survived. These were the people who had preserved their spiritual sight, perhaps by keeping open their crown chakra. The chakras are 'organs' or energy centres in the subtle body that occultists tell us interpenetrates our physical body. The chakras connect us with our spiritual selves and can be opened. Part of the dawning awareness of the age is the growing consciousness of these chakras and practice in opening them. (This technique is explored in *Witchcraft – A Beginner's Guide* and *The Wheel of the Year – Myth and Magic Through the Seasons*. Full information and instructions are given in *Chakras for Beginners*. Please see Further Reading.)

Those who survived emerged into the open air through a reed, from ant cavities underground. This in itself can be seen as a metaphor for 'going up' by means of the crown chakra and echoes the construction of the ceremonial underground chambers of the Native Americans, called *kivas*. The Great Spirit laid out ears of corn for those who came out. The Hopi waited until last and took the smallest ears, thus becoming the chosen people. The Hopi leader had two sons. One was dark-skinned, wise in the ways of nature, but unsophisticated. The other was fair skinned, clever and resourceful, but lacking the depth of reflection. Probably these two offspring symbolise the right and left hemispheres of the brain, synthesis and imagination being the gifts of the right, logic and discrimination the left.

A plan for peace and balance was inscribed on two stone tablets and one was given to each of the brothers. A pair of stone tablets was given to the red, yellow, black and white races. The Tibetans hold the tablets for the yellow race. This is the realm of the south and the guardianship of the wind. Thus these people were to learn about the sky and breathing. The Kikuyu in Kenya hold tablets for the black race, having guardianship of the west and the powerful but humble element of water. The Swiss are holders for the white race, for the north and for fire, for fire lies within most of the white race's creations, from light bulb to internal combustion engine. The white brothers and sisters began to move upon the face of the earth, as fire does, and it falls to them to unite the human family. The Hopi hold one of the tablets for the red race, of the earth and the east. The red people were to learn about herbs, crops and the gifts of the earth. Eight out of ten foods that we eat are developed in the Western Hemisphere. The Hopi are waiting for the 'true white brother' (i.e. the fair-skinned twin) to return with the other tablet. It is significant to note that if you were to go straight through the centre of the earth, from the Hopi reservation, you would emerge in Tibet. The Tibetan word for sun is the Hopi for moon; the Hopi word for sun is the Tibetan for moon.

Each tablet details the special gift of each race as they migrated throughout the world. The Hopi went to the dwelling place of the Great Spirit, in the spiritual centre of the continent. Lasting peace cannot be achieved until red, white, yellow and black people sit in the same circle. There are no red people in the highest councils of the world, as yet, although the twentieth century has seen the creation of the United Nations, where black, white and yellow races sit. However, the prophecies indicate that true peace cannot be cemented until the circle is complete. At the end of the present cycle the tablet holders from the four directions must meet, to share their wisdom. But should these tablets be cast upon the ground, a great whirlwind shall destroy the earth. In other words, if the sacred life-plan is disregarded, holocaust will arrive. The Great Spirit taught the survivors that when the elder white brother returned to the country of the younger, then the Great Purification might be at hand, and that if he came bearing as his symbol a cross within a circle, then he was to be welcomed. However, if he came with only a cross, then the message was to take care, for the time of the Purification was indeed

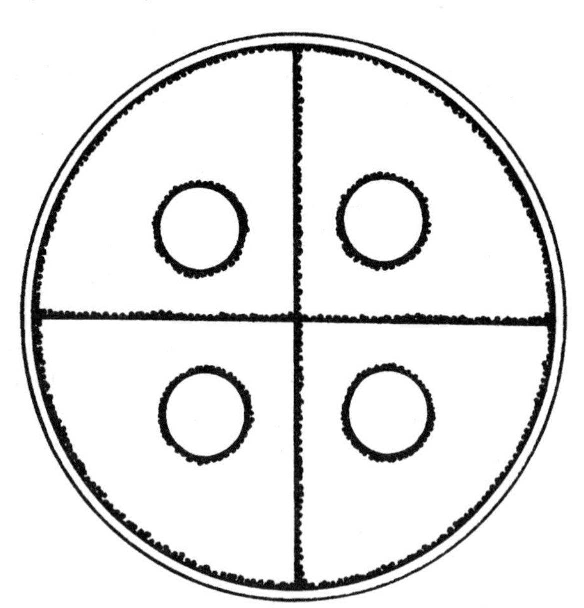

Hopi shield symbol

close. The missionaries, bringing only the cross, were separated from the cycle of creation and the Earth Mother in a religion that was cerebral and dualistic, not bringing balance and understanding.

The Hopi shield symbol portrays a cross within a circle. In each of the quadrants so created, there is a smaller circle. This has many traditional meanings, such as the four directions, the four traditional elements of earth, fire, air and water, the four seasons and others. It signifies the sacred balance of our earthly state. The Hopi inhabit an area known as the 'four corners' where the borders of Utah, Arizona, Colorado and New Mexico meet. The Hopi feel they are keepers of balance and harmony and that their land is especially significant in the planetary scheme.

Hopi life-plan petroglyph

Near Oraibi village in Hopi territory, there is a petroglyph, carved on a rock. It is forbidden to photograph this, so several versions are in circulation, although interpretations coincide. This carving shows the life-plan prophecy. Here we see the bow and arrow, given to the Hopi by the Great Spirit, who holds the reed through which the people emerged. The higher line shows the materialistic lifestyle, the lower line the spiritual path. This is interesting, for we tend to think of the spiritual being 'higher' but this position seems to indicate the need to go within, to honour the earth and to be aware of the sacred in the earth and in daily life – to 'ground' ourselves. On the materialistic path are three figures whose heads do not make contact with their bodies, so are lost in 'head stuff'. These are the whites and Hopi who have adopted their ways. The first vertical line indicates the meeting between whites and Hopi. The first two circles that the lower line passes through are the two world wars, the third circle represents the Great Purification. This last circle comes after the second verticle line, which is our opportunity to change direction. The circle here is unbroken, meaning balance, harmony or a 'cosmic egg'. After this point the materialistic path waivers and fades. Plants are abundant and the figure stands with head firmly on shoulders, integrated and complete, above the shield symbol.

Other prophecies speak of paths in the sky and cobwebs in the air – aeroplanes and transmission lines. A 'gourd of ashes' is foretold that drops on the land, destroying growth for many years and this is reminiscent of the atomic bombs dropped on Hiroshima and Nagasaki, and tested here and there throughout the world. The Hopi realised, when this unholy bomb exploded, that the time of the Great Purification was close at hand and their teachings needed to be circulated. Awareness must spread, or there is a danger that life upon our earth could be wiped out. Hopi teachings indicate signs of each 'world shaking'. The first was a bug moving along a black ribbon, which became identified as a car going along a road, and the first 'shaking' threw the bug into the sky (i.e. it became a plane). With each world shaking the strongest forces survive and build to create the next event. The swastika (which is an ancient symbol of the motion of the sun and cyclical balance), the sun and the colour red are all involved in the prophecy. The third purification is symbolised by the colour red and it will result in the rebuilding of all life, or its total destruction. Some believe that this refers to Eastern people wearing red, for the prophecies say 'the red hat and cloak people will have a huge population'. There are Buddhist red-hat sects who have established centres in the West and a prophecy by the master of the Red Hat sect in the eighth century foretells 'When the iron bird flies, and horses run on wheels, the Tibetan people will be scattered like ants across the world. And the Dharma will come to the land of the red man'. Tibet is a land of immense and incommunicable spiritual insight, that complements the 'earth wisdom' of the red people. In 1979 a lama from the Red Hat sect of Drepung Monastery in India travelled to Hopi land to meet with the elders and to fulfil the prophecy. Much work is being undertaken, behind the scenes, by those who are aware, to lift the earth into her new phase without destruction.

If our culture cannot expand and change to absorb the wisdom teachings, the negative aspects of the prophecies will come to pass, say the Hopi. The colour red will come from the east as destruction. We imagine this as war and violence of the most horrible kind and the colour red is reminiscent of 'red China'. However, a more subtle takeover could be the scenario, for China has been described as a forthcoming 'super presence' rather than 'super-power', in the coming millennium. All too aware of the mistakes made by the West, in terms of economics and 'dependent mentality', Chinese 'takeover' could be commercial. What that might mean is not quite clear, but in the worst scenario it could be depressingly materialistic and/or mean the negation of human rights. There are many possibilities, but it seems we must come together, one way or another, in accord and the sharing of wisdom, or face loss and destruction.

The third purification will be presaged by the dying of trees, a house in the sky, cold places getting hot and hot ones cold, lands rising from beneath the seas and sinking below it, and the appearance of a blue star. With pollution, changing weather due to global warming, sky-lab and space stations and other changes, these are all coming to pass. The blue star did indeed appear as a massive supernova in the Greater Magellanic Cloud, in 1987, at the time of the signing of the Nuclear Arms Limitation Treaty and the Harmonic Convergence, when many people gathered together at special locations to channel and amplify new vibrational frequencies from the galaxy, to bring earth into harmony with the cosmos.

The Hopi believe that their trust is a vital one, and a heavy burden, for their land is regarded as a point of energy balance on the planet. Many people believe that the earth is criss-crossed by an energy network often called ley lines, and that these subtle energies of the living earth can be sensed, dowsed and are amplified at special sites, such as Stonehenge and Avebury in England, and in similar centres worldwide. The Hopi territory would seem especially significant. Human conflicts, mining and other technology disturb the 'serpent power' within the earth. These can be offset by restoring balance at the spiritual nexus, which is Hopi territory. The Hopi have offered their wisdom, their teachings and their help. Instead, the heart has been torn out of their land by strip mining, resulting in fearful pollution and devastation. Of course, nothing can be proven regarding the special nature of the Hopi territory, and it is a belief destined to be regarded with contempt by those out for profit. However, there is evidence to show that the strongest electromagnetic emanations come from the heart and lungs area of the human body. The Four Corners area has more lightning than anywhere else in North America and is the site of the largest energy generating grid in the entire world. However we look at it, the devastation of the Hopi land, a land to which they had ancestral right and to whose inclement conditions they had adapted, is a heartbreaking metaphor for our disregard for the earth, for ancient wisdom teachings, for our own future – in short for anything but a quick buck.

The Hopi did not agree to this incursion into their land. It was allowed by the Hopi Tribal Council, which was foisted upon the Hopi by central government, but the traditional Hopi do not recognise it. The Hopi could never relinquish the sacred trust given to them by the Great Spirit at the dawning of our time. Hopi sacred sites and ritual centres have been desecrated. Many people believe that grave damage has been done to the planetary grid, that grid of ley lines, or the energy web of Spider Woman who assisted the Great Spirit. Nothing can be done to convince those who do not wish to see regarding what is being done to the earth, and that more is being destroyed than tradition and homeland, as if that were not enough. Only when the rivers have run dry, the last tree has been felled, the last bird has been shot and the last rich acre pillaged for profit, will the white race realise that you can't eat money!

EDGAR CAYCE

Called the 'Sleeping Prophet' from his ability to make predictions when in a state of self-hypnosis, Edgar Cayce was an otherwise ordinary American, born on a Kentucky farm in 1877 and living until 1945. He taught Sunday School and was devoted to his family. He found some of his trance statements shocking, as he was a devout Christian, but he came to accept the idea of reincarnation. As a child he displayed an impressive photographic memory when he slept with his schoolbooks under his head. However, his true talents did not emerge until, as an adult, he was threatened with the loss of his voice through paralysis of the throat. Cayce recalled his sleep-learning faculties, asked a friend to give him a hypnotic suggestion and placed himself in a trance. While in the trance he was able to prescribe a cure – it seems he was unconsciously longing to give up his job as a salesman and the cause of his voice loss was psychological. In itself that is a classic scenario and not remarkable, but Cayce's abilities extended much further. Soon he was diagnosing and prescribing for people all over the country, using medical words that he did not understand in his normal consciousness. His abilities developed, extending to clairvoyance and prophecy and resulting in a vast body of interrelated readings.

Cayce's predictions encompass all levels – international relations, scientific advancement, environmental change and the growth in spirituality of the human race. They include: food scarcity, due to geographic upheaval; Japan will be lost beneath the sea and the upper portion of Europe changed radically; many of the battlefields of the Second World War are to become ocean; open waters are to appear in Greenland and South America will be shaken from end to end; Los Angeles, San Francisco and New York are all to disappear. Cayce also predicts the Big One – an enormous earthquake along the San Andreas fault that scientists have been awaiting for some time. Cayce predicted a pole shift around 2000–2001. According to him the New Age began in 1931. Certain of Cayce's predictions have been impressive; for example he predicted that two American presidents would die in office (which happened to Kennedy and Roosevelt) and that a community called the Essenes lived near the Dead Sea, which was verified by the discovery of the Dead Sea scrolls, two years after Cayce's death.

Some of Cayce's most interesting revelations concern Atlantis which, despite the fact many people view the entire idea of the lost continent with scepticism, will not go away. He said Atlantis occupied a place in what is now the Atlantic Ocean from the Sargasso Sea to the Azores. The civilisation flourished from 200,000 BCE and was highly developed, possessing a 'crystal stone' that could trap the rays of the sun. But the Atlanteans became corrupt and the continent was finally destroyed around 10,000 BCE. However, many of the Atlanteans had dispersed across the globe. Cayce foretold that Atlantis would begin to rise again in the area of the Bimini Islands in the Bahamas in 1968–9. New lands, he said, would appear in the Pacific and Atlantic, among them Poseidon, apparently one of the five residual islands from underwater Atlantis. In fact, archaeologists discovered part of this island off one of the Bimini Islands in 1974, as Cayce had foretold. Cayce also said that documents that proved the existence of Atlantis would be found in a chamber underneath the Sphinx in Egypt: the Hall of Records, which holds the history of the earth, will be found in the right paw of the Sphinx. While the Sphinx was being renovated in the mid-1990s the right shoulder kept breaking open and the head also threatened to fall off. In *Nothing In This Book Is True, But It's Exactly How Things Are* (see Further Reading), Bob Frissell tells us that a golden sphere, which is, in fact, a time capsule, will be found in the neck of the Sphinx. It is unclear whether the Hall of Records has, in fact, been discovered already. It apparently contains information on many different dimensional levels and, if this is the case, it is the key and the entry to a totally different phase of consciousness for humankind. The Giza plateau is the focus for many stories, some of them apparently fantastical, and the jury is still out.

Cayce has been vaunted as an accurate prophet. However, many of his predictions were so vague as to be meaningless and some were plain wrong. For instance, he said that

Spanish troubles were only just beginning when, in fact, the civil war was drawing to a close and Franco's regime was set to bring many decades of peace, followed by smooth, transition to democracy. Like many prophets he was obscure, saying of Britain that it would be able to control the world for peace 'when its activities are set in such a way as to bring consideration of every phrase . . .'. It would certainly be nice to think that following on from days of empire and conquest, Britain might be a beacon for tolerance, fairness and balance. Cayce predicted that great cataclysms would afflict the earth from 1958 to the end of the twentieth century. As I write there are less than two years to go for this to be fulfilled.

Like all prophets, Cayce seems to have spoken in allegory at times. However, the most important point is that the job of prophets is to warn. Contemporary seers indicate that a change in mass consciousness has come into effect and that this has averted some of the worst scenarios. Certainly things have changed. There was a time when nationalism and patriotism were prime motivators and it would be rare for people to speak openly against a war that purported to protect the security of the nation. Things are different now and people are not so readily convinced that 'fighting for peace' is a realistic possibility. This is not confined to a handful of idealists, but goes across all races and classes. Some psychics have reported that the huge numbers of dead in the two world wars have acted as a sort of communal sacrifice that has helped to raise the level of consciousness, and that their forgiveness and their influence from the spirit plane means that we can move onwards as a species. A channelled message by the psychic Eddie Burks (excerpted from *Ghosthunter* by Burks and Cribbs, Headline, 1995) tells us:

> *History presents many sad examples of cruel massacres . . . Romans . . . Ghengis Khan – right up to the present tragedies in the Balkans and Rwanda . . . the victims of these massacres . . . are able to forgive the*

people who caused their deaths. Through this act of forgiveness, they transmute the pain of their suffering into a love of humanity . . . and by doing so they raise humanity on earth one small – but very significant – step upwards, towards the spirit world . . . suffering on such a scale is never wasted, either for the individual or for humanity.

THE BIBLE

Alone among ancient texts, the Bible is often taken literally, in the Western world, by people who are sceptical about everything else. The Bible has been translated and re-translated many times. It was added to as recently as 1611 by King James I of England, VI of Scotland, who wrote 'Thou shalt not suffer a witch to live' (Exodus 22:18). James was a paranoid monarch, who saw dark threat everywhere. One of the most noticeable biblical 'mistakes' is in the use of the word 'virgin' which means a woman untouched by man and physically intact. The original Hebrew does not contain this inference and a virgin would, therefore, be a woman who was self-possessed, possibly entering into sexual relations if she chose, but belonging to no man, in the tradition of the temple virgins (who, by some accounts, were explicitly *not* intact virgins!). The patriarchal Bible is often not friendly to women and sexual equality, and as a role-model, the tyrannical, vengeful Yahweh of the Old Testament – by his own description 'jealous' – leaves much to be desired. Contradictions abound in the Bible. Where, at one point we are exhorted to 'take an eye for an eye', in the New Testament Jesus tells us to 'turn the other cheek'. It is hard to see how the Bible can be designated categorically as the word of God when it is so obviously the word of man (and I mean 'man' and explicitly not 'woman'). None the less, the Bible enshrines wisdom and prophecy that may be relevant to us today.

The Old Testament prophets, the reported words of Christ and the book of Revelation all contain prophecy. The Day of Judgment and the end of the world are indicated, but this does not necessarily mean total annihilation, but the end of the world order as we know it. Naturally much biblical prophecy is couched in terms that belong to the prophets' own times, but that does not mean that they are not a metaphor for what can happen in our time.

> *Alas for the day! for the day of the Lord is at hand, and as a destruction from the Almighty shall it come . . .*
>
> *The seed is rotten under their clods, the garners are laid desolate, the barns are broken down; for the corn is withered . . .*
>
> *O Lord, to thee will I cry: for the fire hath devoured the pastures of the wilderness, and the flame hath burned all the trees of the field.*

JOEL 1:15–19

Such passages can be taken to mean pollution and atomic devastation as a judgment on us for our tampering with Nature, or they can be taken, by die-hards, as a warning of what will happen if we do not live good, pure lives in accordance with the Scriptures. One can only say that if the good Lord's coming is going to be so harsh and unpleasant, it would be better if He took His time! Here there is little evidence of a loving God. Some passages seem to describe literal events:

> *The sun shall be turned into darkness, and the moon into blood, before the great and the terrible day of the Lord come.*

JOEL 2:31

> *. . . I will cause the sun to go down at noon, and I will darken the earth in the clear day.*

AMOS 8:9

This sounds like an eclipse, for the moon does 'turn to blood' in an eclipse and total solar eclipse brings darkness in the day. Solar and lunar eclipses occur in the same month, within about a fortnight of each other, and were always considered dire portents.

> *And I will turn your feasts into mourning, and all your songs into lamentation; and I will bring up sackcloth upon all loins, and baldness upon every head; and I will make it as the mourning of an only son, and the end thereof a bitter day.*
>
> *. . . I will send a famine in the land, not a famine of bread nor a thirst for water, but of hearing the words of the Lord.*
>
> AMOS 8:10–11

Such prophecies have been linked to important eclipses such as that scheduled for August 1999, discussed in Chapter 2, and we could be forgiven for linking them to radiation sickness and similar. Certainly spiritual impoverishment is indicated in the last two lines, and that does seem a reality in our times. These passages make such gloomy reading they are guaranteed to foster a guilt complex and millenarian anxiety. We link them to our time, but so have many people in history made links with their own time and seen it as a time of destruction and loss of spiritual values. The messages of Jesus were much gentler.

The most obviously prophetic section of the Bible is the book of Revelation of Saint John the Divine, describing apocalyptic future events and telling of the second coming of Christ. This is most complex and metaphorical. Here it is possible for us to take only snippets.

One of the most striking parts of Revelation is John's account of a scroll with seven seals, each revealing an aspect of retribution that will arrive before the last judgment.

> *And I saw in the right hand of him that sat on the throne a book written within and on the back-side, sealed with seven seals.*
>
> *And I saw a strong angel proclaiming with a loud voice, Who is worthy to open the book, and to loose the seals thereof?*
>
> *And no man in heaven, nor in earth, neither under the earth, was able to open the book, neither to look thereon.*
>
> REVELATION 5:1–3

Then a Lamb appears 'as it has been slain' with seven horns and seven eyes 'which are the seven Spirits of God' (5:6). The Lamb proceeds to open the seven seals one by one. Moria Timms in *Prophecies To Take You Into the 21st Century* (see Further Reading) makes the important point that the seven seals are allegories for each of the seven chakras, which are energy centres connecting the physical body with the spiritual bodies. She writes:

> *With the opening of each seal comes 'revelation' and the opportunity to be purified and transformed by the particular energies released. The more successful we are in handling and transmuting within ourselves . . . the intense surge of purifying energy released by the opening of each seal, the less necessary it is for these releases to manifest in the external world as chaos and catastrophe.*

With the opening of the first four seals those well-known villains the Four Horsemen of the Apocalypse, war, famine, pestilence and death come out to play. With the opening of the chakras (please see Further Reading for books on the chakras), the kundalini energy coiled at the base of the spine is awakened and rises through the spiritual centres. However, some have warned that the kundalini can run in reverse, resulting in extreme sexuality and the abuse of the power that has been aroused. This may be what the four horsemen signify. Perhaps they also signify the challenges that must be overcome by awakening humanity, for no one whose chakras are opened can turn away their face from the suffering that exists all over the globe, or deny that we are all responsible, in some form.

After the opening of the sixth seal, we are told:

> *And the heaven departed as a scroll when it is rolled together; and every mountain and island were moved out of their places.*
>
> REVELATION 6:14

Moira Timms links this to pole shift, which has been foretold in many prophecies. Later on it is written:

> *And there fell upon men a great hail out of heaven, every stone about the weight of a talent: and men blasphemed God because of the plague of the hail; for the plague thereof was exceeding great.*
>
> REVELATION 16:21

This Moira Timms feels refers to 'the meteor showers or the tektites that have been scientifically recorded during past geomantic reversals' – bearing in mind that a talent weighed around 34 kg (75 lb).

Revelation continues with a pause as the elect are sealed in the foreheads. In the forehead is the sixth chakra which relates to intuition and a sense of profound knowing. This chakra has been linked to the 'third eye' and the pineal gland. It is the doorway to the higher consciousness of the seventh or crown chakra, through which the spiritual light floods the awakened being – the 'many-petalled lotus' of enlightenment. Moira Timms links Jesus with the doorway to the spirit:

Behold I stand at the door and knock; if any man hear my voice and open the door, I will come in to him . . . Jesus said;

. . . I am the way, the truth, and the life: no man cometh unto the Father, but by me.

JOHN 14:6

This statement has been taken literally and millions have been tortured and burnt alive, whole nations have been put to the sword and vast libraries and storehouses of ancient knowledge destroyed forever. Many people believe that this was no part of Christ's meaning, indeed it must surely be the opposite of His intention! Jesus Christ, as shaman and teacher, was surely pointing out that the only way to true spirituality was to awaken these abilities within ourselves, so that only by cultivating our spiritual awareness and arousing the 'Christ-consciousness' within can we progress, as a species, in the way of love and truth. Thus no one comes to the father other than through the internal 'Christ' or awakened Self. Again, I turn to Moira Timms:

The universal force which is the radiant consciousness of the Christ guides the 'Way', reveals the 'Truth', and en'Light'ens our minds that we may fulfil our evolutionary destiny, become Christed, inherit the Kingdom. That's what the New Age is folks!

As Revelation progresses other tribulations are foretold that can now be linked to modern warfare, pollution and such like, for instance:

And the shape of the locusts were like unto horses prepared unto battle; . . .

And they had breastplates as it were breastplates of iron; and the sound of their wings was as the sound of chariots . . .

And they had tails like unto scorpions; . . . and their power was to hurt men five months.

REVELATION 9:7–10

Could these be helicopters, bearing some form of germ warfare? Or are we here warned about insect plagues which are indeed arriving due to environmental imbalance and the over-use of pesticides? Many other afflictions are foretold, that could mean skin cancers, nuclear warfare, natural disasters of unparalleled magnitude and other tasty morsels. Most utterances could be interpreted in many different ways.

Revelation 12 tells of a woman 'clothed with the sun, and the moon under her feet, and upon her head a crown of twelve stars' (12:1). This woman is ready to give birth, but she is persecuted by a dragon with seven heads and ten horns. The woman escapes:

And to the woman were given two wings of a great eagle, that she might fly into the wilderness, into her place, where she is nourished . . .

And the earth helped the woman, and the earth opened her mouth, and swallowed up the flood which the dragon cast out of his mouth.

REVELATION 12:14–16

I cannot help wondering if this passage refers to the persecution and exile of Goddess-consciousness and true respect for the Feminine principle.

The thirteenth chapter unfolds with the apparition of a beast with ten horns. This has been linked to the European Union, which used to have ten members, or the ten-nation Arab Confederacy. A corrupt world system is here indicated. Along comes another beast 'and causeth the earth and them which dwell therein to worship the first beast'

(13:12). Here we have the anti-hero to outdo all others, the Antichrist.

> *And that no man might buy or sell, save that he had the mark, or the name of the beast, or the number of his name.*
>
> *Here is wisdom. Let him that hath understanding count the number of the beast: for it is the number of man: and his number is six hundred three-score and six.*
>
> 13:17–18

This Antichrist will appear as a saviour and he will be supported by a false prophet. We are warned not to believe those who can do wonders, for they are not necessarily spiritual beings. Some have likened the New Age movement and its gurus to the coming of false prophets. However, I do not think we have to look far for the Antichrist, for he seems alive and well in many institutions that have chosen to interpret the gospels literally, going quite against spiritual direction by becoming preoccupied with the historical Christ and his body and barring the way to exploration and growth, as the Vatican has been accused of doing, with its monopoly on the Dead Sea scrolls. Religious orthodoxy and material wealth can be seen as two sides of the same coin, and that coin is temporal power. Perhaps it is the currency of the Beast.

Better things are foretold in the closing chapters of Revelation.

> *And God shall wipe away all tears from their eyes; and there shall be no more death, neither sorrow, not crying, neither shall there be any more pain: for the former things are passed away.*
>
> *And he that sat upon the throne said, Behold, I make all things new.*
>
> 21:4–5

> *And he shewed me a pure river of water of life, clear as crystal . . .*
>
> *In the midst of the street of it, and on either side of the river, was there the tree of life, which bare twelve manner of fruits, and yielded her fruit every month: and the leaves of the tree were for the healing of the nations.*
>
> 22:1–2

Here a new world order is presaged and much better times. It is irresistible to link the tree of life with 12 fruits yielded monthly to the 12 astrological signs through which the sun passes, indicating 12 basic modes of earthly manifestation and linked by astrologers to human personality, earthly events, etc. This is not to say that sun-sign astrology comes as a salvation to the earth, but perhaps a realisation of our connection to the cosmos, of a 'wholeness' in heaven and earth and a concept of a progressive cycle, wisdom attained through observation of our place in the scheme of things is the hint. Here we are in the next phase of our evolution. The second coming of Christ that is foretold, and which we are warned will be deceptively aped by the Antichrist, occurs within ourselves when we make the transition to universal consciousness, to a Christ consciousness that moves beyond the small self and sees the greater Self everywhere, with love.

All this may sound terribly exalted. To become God's elect we have to be sealed on our foreheads, all our chakras open, extremely advanced spiritual beings, etc. I do not think it is quite like that or that 'salvation' is open only to those who sit in the lotus position for hours each day and harp on about enlightenment, any more than I believe that being chosen is a matter of attending church and refraining from impure thoughts. Rather, it seems, we are called to open our eyes and our hearts, to become global citizens, conscious of more than our own wishes and ends, not blindly accepting or judging, fostering our own inner power to act and decide and not seeking power over others. Something has to give in the status quo, or so it seems the prophecies indicate. Those who feel it truly as 'fire and brimstone' will possibly be those who have most to lose, who are the most deeply addicted and have the most invested in things as they are. It's a big, beautiful world and it belongs to us all. Let's wake up and get a life!

NOSTRADAMUS

Nostradamus was the Latinised name of Michel de Notredame, a French prophet and seer who was born in 1503 under the sign of Capricorn, at the winter solstice, and died in 1566. His name has become synonymous with prophecy, but there was much more to his life. Nostradamus was a qualified doctor, author of philosophical treatises, writer on food and cosmetics and adviser to the queen of France. Apparently a kindly, generous and brave man, who also possessed a sense of humour, Nostradamus was known as a plague doctor who risked his life to treat the victims of this dreadful sickness. He was controversial in that he did not bleed his patients, insisting on fresh air and running water, rather than well water. Of Jewish ancestry, he was a 'wandering Jew' for much of his life, having tragically lost his attractive wife and two small children in a plague. Because his family died, Nostradamus was regarded as a failure, despite all the lives he had saved, and his patrons deserted him. His best and influential friend quarrelled with him, his dead wife's family sued for the return of her dowry and the Inquisition summoned him for questioning. Nostradamus was no stranger to tragedy, loneliness and fear.

In 1547 Nostradamus married again and from this time his life was happy and settled. He and his wife had many children and he had the opportunity to study the occult and write his Almanacks, which were a success, despite the fact that many of his predictions were wrong. However, he was summoned to court and kept the favour of the queen, Catharine de Medici, having foretold the death in a duel of her husband Henri. This event was also predicted by the astrologer Luc Gauric and came to pass because Henri had no time for prophets and took no notice. However, this accurate prediction made a name for Nostradamus.

Many stories are told about Nostradamus that illustrate his talent for prophecy. While in Ancona in Italy he met a young swineherd called Felix Peretti. Nostradamus knelt in the road as the boy passed and when questioned about this he replied 'I must kneel before His Holiness'. Peretti became Pope Sixtus V, 20 years after the death of Nostradamus. Another account tells how a friend whose hospitality Nostradamus was enjoying asked him to predict the fate of two piglets, whereupon the prophet said that a wolf would eat the white one and they would have the black one at table. Intent on some sport, his host told the cook to kill the white one. However, a tame wolf-cub gnawed the prepared pig, so the cook took the black one, cooked it and served it. His host confronted Nostradamus with the fact they were eating the white pig, but Nostradamus insisted it was the black pig. Eventually, the cook owned up and confirmed that Nostradamus was correct! Another charming tale tells how the prophet met a young girl walking towards the woods one evening. '*Bonjour fillette*', he said. Meeting her again on her way back he greeted her with a smile '*Bonjour petite femme*'. He knew quite well what she had been doing in the woods!

The 'Prophecies' of Nostradamus are extensive. They were intended to be a series of 1,000 predictions, divided into books containing 100 centaines or quatrains. 'Centaine' does not refer to a century of time, but a set of 100 predictions. The seventh century contains only 42 quatrains, so possibly Nostradamus died before they were

complete. These prophecies were intended to contain predictions right up to the end of the world. Nostradamus was a 'Millennium man' believing that the world would end in 2000, or possibly 3000. The Church had confidently predicted the end of the world in the year 1000, to the extent that people left their fields and animals untended, awaiting the Last Day. When this did not materialise, it took at least two years for things to get back to normal. The Church simply shifted its prediction to the year 2000; this had tremendous influence, even on cultured and educated men of the sixteenth century, such as Nostradamus. Nostradamus was also influenced by the Old Testament and expected false prophets and religions, revolution, war, famine, despoiling of the earth (pollution), earthquakes and plagues. He was not optimistic about our chances! However, with Nostradamus it is easy to be wise after the event. The quatrains are mostly cryptic and can be linked to events that have taken place, but it is harder to be sure about the future.

Certain quatrains were stunningly accurate. One that predicts the death of the French king Henri II runs:

> *The young lion will overcome the old, in a field of combat in a single fight. He will pierce his eyes in a golden cage, two wounds in one, he then dies a cruel death.*

Henri insisted on jousting and both he and his young opponent wore a lion on their coat of arms. Montgomery, who rode against the king, knew of the prediction and did not want to joust, but the king insisted. Montgomery's lance slipped and pierced the king's gold helmet and entered his head just above the eye. Some reports also state he was wounded in the throat; he died in agony ten days later.

Quatrain IX.C runs:

> *A naval battle will be overcome at night. Fire in the ruined strips of the West. A new coding, the great ship*

> *coloured with anger to the vanquished. Victory in a mist.*

This is taken to mean the Japanese attack on Pearl Harbor early one morning in 1941, drawing the United States into the Second World War – a new type of warmongering attack, bringing anger finally to a Japan defeated by a sudden and even more terrible attack, the bombs on Hiroshima and Nagasaki, hazy glimpses of victory to the United States.

Quatrain IX. LXVI runs:

> *He will be taken to the corner of Luna where he will be placed on foreign land. The unripe fruit will be the subject of great scandal. Great blame, to the others great praise.*

This is interpreted as referring to the Moon landing in 1969, to the explosion of Space Shuttle *Challenger* in 1986 and to the success of the Russian space station *Mir*.

Quatrain V.XXIX runs:

> *Liberty will not be regained. It will be occupied by a black, proud, villainous and unjust man. When the subject of the Pope is opened by Hister, the republic of Venice will be angered.*

This is taken as speaking of Mussolini's plans to make an alliance with Hitler between 1934 and 1938. They meet in Venice. 'Black' may refer to the Fascists, the Blackshirts or to Hitler. The Pope played an important part in the scenario and refused to excommunicate either Hitler or Mussolini, or to condemn the German invasion of Poland. The Vatican was an escape route for German war criminals.

Nostradamus is believed to have foretold frequent earthquakes during the eighth and ninth decades of the twentieth century, unrest in the Middle East, the last British monarch to reign, the coming of the third Antichrist

(Napoleon and Hitler being numbers one and two), the AIDS epidemic and a Third World War, followed by a lasting peace. As an example, quatrain VI.XCVII is one that has not yet been fulfilled, and it tells us

> *The sky will burn at 45 degrees. Fire approaches the great New City. Immediately a huge scattered flame leaps up when they want to have proof of the Normans.*

This has been taken to mean the destruction of New York, lying between the 40th and 45th parallels. France ('the Normans') is involved, apparently.

An example of how hard it can be to arrive at an interpretation of Nostradamus comes with this scary quatrain, X.LXXII:

> *L'an mil neuf cens nonante neuf sept mois,*
> *Du ciel viendra un grand Roy deffraieur*
> *Resusciter le grand Roy d'Angolmois.*
> *Avant apres Mars regner par bon heur.*

I have seen two different translations, as follows:

> *The year 1999, seventh month,*
> *A great king of terror will descend from the skies*
> *To resuscitate the great king of Angolmois,*
> *Around this time Mars will reign for the good cause.*

and

> *In the year 1999 and seven months, from the sky will come the great King of Terror. He will bring to life the great king of the Mongols. Before and after war reigns happily.*

The first translation has been suggested as possibly presaging the liberation of Phobos, satellite of Mars (whose name means 'terror') who comes careering towards the earth, causing great catastrophe. The second has been taken as the coming of the Third Antichrist in July 1999. This Antichrist is the king of the Mongols, arriving before the final advent of the great King of Terror. This translation depends on 'Angolmois' being an anagram of the Old French 'Mongolois', which it isn't, exactly. The line '*Du ciel viendra un grand Roy deffraieur*' may also refer to the arrival of powerful extra-terrestrials.

It seems to me likely that Nostradamus, astrologer and seer of the sixteenth century, by 'Mars' meant exactly the astronomical/astrological Mars, and he may just possibly have been aware of the planetary configuration that coincides with the eclipse in August 1999, as discussed previously, although it is most unlikely he would have been able to predict the eclipse itself by contemporary methods. The Grand Cross of Saturn, Mars, Uranus and the Sun is actually at its closest to exactitude several days before the eclipse date. In the old Julian calender that predates our present Gregorian dating, this would fall in the seventh month (i.e. July), as would the eclipse itself because the use of the Julian calendar for the twentieth century would result in an error of 13 days. Any astrologer with millenarian expectations, weighted by medieval fatedness and Old Testament fears of retribution would see this Grand Cross, in such a fateful year, as alarming! Because of the importance of the millennium it may be possible that the seer worked out these planetary cycles and worked from them for this prediction. However, if he did not, in a sense it renders the prediction more significant – and unsettling.

While some of the prophecies of Nostradamus are impressive, others are obscure and even meaningless, while still others seem to refer to events that were already past in the time of the prophet or even to legends of classical mythology. Some have said that Nostradamus was spot on up until the 1970s but since then he has been adrift, and this may be put down to an evolution in human consciousness, which has kept some of the disasters at bay.

If so, his warnings have been heeded. I do not believe that judgment on us has been suspended so much as by our thoughts, beliefs and expectations we are 'making our own luck'. Many people are consciously sending out love towards the entire planet, and in many countries nationalistic fervour is at an all-time low, with ordinary folk simply feeling that war is not and can never be the answer. Whatever the case may be, the predictions of Nostradamus are shrouded in mystique, and it seems to me that even the examples given, which are regarded as 'good' quatrains, could be interpreted very differently. For example, the name Hitler is spelt 'Hister' by Nostradamus, and some interpreters have argued that it doesn't mean Hitler at all. It seems that one needs to be something of a seer oneself to interpret Nostradamus!

THE PROPHECIES OF ST MALACHY

St Malachy, an Irish saint, was Bishop of Armagh in Northern Ireland, in the twelfth century. His prophecies concerning the popes were published in Venice in 1595 by the Dominican monk Arnold de Wion, in his *Lignum Vitae*. The record of the prophecies, according to De Wion, was kept in the Vatican for 500 years. The Vatican censors examined all material before it was printed, thus suggesting historical authenticity. St Malachy's prophecies have proved strikingly accurate, although he is by no means well-known as a prophet. St Bernard de Clairvaux, his intimate friend, wrote about St Malachy and testified to his gifts. St Malachy died in St Bernard's arms in 1148. It is a significant fact that St Bernard was one of the founders of the Order of the Temple. The Knights Templar are believed to have had access to esoteric knowledge, gained in the East and to have developed occult powers, because of which the Church later persecuted them for heresy. There may be more than meets the eye behind the abilities of St Malachy.

He predicted momentous events for the end of the twentieth century and it is undeniable that the ending of the Papacy would be a highly significant matter, politically and spiritually.

The prophecies that concern us relate to the final popes. St Malachy named the last pope as Petro Romano, Peter the Roman. As it has been estimated that the average reign of each pope lasts about eight years, the ending of the Papacy is indicated in the opening years of the twenty-first century. The last four popes are identified as:

1 DE MEDIETATE LUNAE or CONCERNING THE HALF-MOON This can be taken to mean the reign of Albino Luciani, Pope John Paul 1st, whose name signifies the white light of the waxing moon and who died after three weeks in office, his period of effective power this spanning only a half-moon of two weeks.

2 DE LABORE SOLIS or OF THE LABOUR OF THE SUN This is taken to refer to the present (1998) Pope, John Paul 2nd, whose labours take him into many Third World tropical and sub-tropical countries, which are the only locations where Catholicism is on the increase. Of course, this may also refer to increased solar activity in regard to sunspots, or even to the integrative, creative function of the sun in an astrological chart.

3 DE GLORIA OLIVAE – THE GLORY OF THE OLIVE This is taken to refer to a black pope.

4 PETRO ROMANO or PETER THE ROMAN These cryptic lines could be interpreted several ways, for instance, DE GLORIA OLIVAE may refer to the olive branch, traditional symbol of peace. Peter the Roman is predicted by St Malachy to rule in the midst of tribulations which culminate in the destruction of the Papacy.

While St Malachy's prophecies are impressive, there are lines that could be interpreted several ways and, naturally, it is easy to be wise after the event. For instance, PASTOR ANGELICUS obviously relates to the 'Angelic Pope' Pius XII, who was a mystic, reigning from 1939–58. An earlier prediction, RELIGIO DEPOPULATA, or DEPOPULATED RELIGION, stands for Benedict XV who reigned from 1914–22, when millions of Christians were killed in the First World War and the Russian Revolution cut Russia off from Christianity. However, while the later FLOS FLORUM is seen to refer to Pius VI who ascended to the Papacy in 1963, there is doubt about the exact connection, which may refer to the Pope's coat of arms, displaying lilies. St Malachy's accuracy concerning the final two popes will be confirmed or otherwise in the new millennium.

POLE SHIFT

Pole shift has apparently been predicted, or hinted at, in several prophecies, so it is worth taking a closer glance at the subject and its physical basis. Substantial, sudden movement of the poles of revolution of the earth would result in winds of unimaginable ferocity, tidal waves so high their crests would be out of sight, oceans turning into mountains and mountains being swallowed beneath the waves. There are many records, in myth or on fragments of faded papyrus, that tell of giant cataclysms that wiped out whole cultures in some dim-and-distant epoch. Geological evidence does suggest that there have been reversals of the poles many times in the past. The great deserts of the world do not lie in the hottest regions, but in areas north and south of the (present) equator. There are indications that the Ice Ages did not creep slowly but came almost instantaneously, and evidence that oceans worldwide rose 60 metres (200 feet) about 13,000 years ago (approximately contemporary to the biblical flood) does exist. Fossils of whales have been found several hundred feet above sea level and hundreds of miles inland, in North

America. Preserved bodies of mammoth herds, with vegetation still in their mouths have been found in the frozen depths of north-east Siberia. Millions of animals such as horse and bison have been mined out of stream valleys in Alaska, all mangled and mixed up with uprooted trees. These factors all suggest a global disaster of mind-boggling magnitude, rather than a stately southwards glide of ice caps.

While acceptance of pole reversal is not universal, the wandering of the magnetic poles is established fact. Opinions are divided as to whether pole reversal coincided with magnetic reversals or whether it happened independently. Since 1950, when volcanic activity apparently increased on earth, the north magnetic pole has moved more than 320 km (200 miles) in contrast with its average motion of 3 km (2 miles) per year over the previous 100 years. As the earth revolves it generates a magnetic field along its axis of rotation, which radiates energy and acts also as a magnet, by this process deflecting cosmic rays from the surface. The strength of this field depends on several factors, including the speed of rotation and the cycles of the sun. Sunspots have marked effects and since 1957 the number of sunspots in solar cycles has been increasing, making 1990 a bumper year. As this cycle takes roughly 11 years, the turn of the millennium could be interesting in this regard.

By examining excavated pottery fragments and rocks, 171 reversals of the magnetic poles have been detected. This evidence arises from iron oxides in igneous rock that acquire a magnetic orientation when they cool, that corresponds to the polarity of the earth at the given time. This indicates that the last reversal occurred 12,400 years ago with a brief anomaly in the ninth century BCE. The evidence suggests that the magnetic charge was at times much, much greater and it has been postulated that in the past the earth may have revolved more quickly. Over the past 1,800 years the magnetic field of the earth has been calculated as having fallen to less than two-thirds its original power. Reversals in the magnetic field were presaged by declines in its strength. In the last 100 years the magnetic field intensity has decreased by over 10 per cent. More radiation is thus falling on earth. It is thought that reduction or elimination of the magnetic field accompanied pole reversal, so many life forms were destroyed by radiation. Atomic clocks confirm that the rotational rate of the earth is indeed slowing, by as much as a second a year, which may not sound much but is significant, scientifically.

No one is sure why the magnetic poles reversed but there are several theories, including collision or close passage with other celestial bodies such as comets or meteorites (or the escaped satellites of other planets, such as Phobos mentioned above, which has the inconvenient habit of revolving centrifugally and thus straining like a mad dog on the leash). Scientists confirm that large meteorites fell like rain at other times of pole reversal, which coincides with prophecy and historical accounts of past catastrophes. Over the aeons the reversals have increased, sometimes having an interval of only 10,000 years between them, and some scientists believe that a shift is overdue. Earthquakes affect the pole of rotation. Hopi myth tells of twin beings who keep the world turning at each of the poles. At the end of the 'Third World' they were told by the Great Spirit to leave their places, after which the earth rolled over twice and a new world came into being. Edgar Cayce told that the northern parts of the earth were once tropical. Science, myth and prophecy all have something to say about reversal of the poles.

It may seem as if we can do nothing to help ourselves, if the poles reverse. However, this may not be the case. Simply, if there are instabilities in the movements of the earth, our tampering with the environment is highly likely to make things worse. Many people believe that earth has a nervous system made up of ley lines, or lines of energy, that criss-cross the surface of the planet. These converge in nodes of special significance sensed by the ancients and marked by structures such as stone circles or the pyramids. This planetary grid can also be correlated to the etheric or 'energy body' that psychics confirm sheaths the physical body of humans in a web of light fibres, and forms a connection to the spiritual or subtle bodies. This grid has been disrupted by the detonation of atomic bombs. If you doubt this grid exists, it is still reasonable to assume that such gross assaults on the delicate balance of nature are asking for trouble – and that trouble could be a pole shift. We would be advised to stop attacking the earth, if for no better reason than that we cannot be sure exactly what we are doing. Chaos theory teaches that tiny factors can influence extensively a large pattern, such as the well-known example of the beating of a butterfly's wings eventually producing a hurricane. We cannot map large variable systems such as the ecosphere. Perhaps we should cease relentlessly interfering and start watching, listening and learning.

Many people believe that planetary events can be influenced by the mass psyche. In other words, what we all think, how we react, what we believe, and what forms our sense of reality affects that reality. Sounds incredible? Quantum physics is beginning to confirm that processes are, indeed, affected by an observer. An example of this is found by shining a beam of light through a pinhole, causing a small circle of light to shine on a screen. If two such pinholes are located side by side, two interlinked circles of light are generated, but the part that overlaps contains some dark lines due to 'interference' between the two beams. If the strength of the beam is then reduced, allowing only one photon (or light energy particle) to pass through at a time one would expect these interference lines to disappear, because single-file photons cannot interfere with each other. However, the interference lines do not disappear. Yet when the photons are monitored, with a photon detector, to find out exactly what is happening at the holes, the interference lines disappear.

In addition, incidences of psychokinesis are well documented. Mind power is a reality. Of course, this doesn't mean that we can harm someone just be hating them. However, it may mean that the positioning of something in the mind-map of millions of people can have an effect in the 'real' world (it's worth remembering here that philosophers have debated the nature of reality for ages). It can also mean that by deliberately concentrating on something and willing it to happen, results may be obtained. Fairy story? That is the usual view. However, it is interesting to note that there was a massive jerk in the earth's magnetic field originating from within the core that took place in 1969, the year humans first walked on the surface of the moon, viewing the earth from space. Perhaps earth has a consciousness, perhaps we are part of that consciousness, interacting with it and affecting it. Of one thing I am absolutely sure: human beings are capable of far more than they believe, and it is belief, or lack of it, that keeps us in check. I have seen one of my sons bend a spoon through stroking it, after watching Uri Geller on television. Geller made him believe he could do it and so he did it with ease. What else might we be able to accomplish? Maybe we should stop erecting our own barriers.

ABOUT PROPHECY

Always we assume that prophecy is about prediction and that a good prophet tells it like it is, or will be. Prediction is more properly understood as small-scale prophecy, telling what will happen in the lives of individuals. Prophecy is on a grander, often global scale. However, the job description of the prophet doesn't include sitting back saying 'I told you so'. If that happens the prophet has failed. Prophets are sent to arouse, awaken, disquiet, prod, warn and promote evolution. The prophet, if she or he is a good one, taps into mass undercurrents and, as these can rarely be rendered literally, the prophet usually speaks in metaphor. That really gets us going! While we are trying to decipher prophecies we may surprise ourselves by our own wisdom, or stymie ourselves by our folly. However, the intention of the prophet is not purposely to confuse. As the mouthpiece of something greater she or he can only give voice to visions and these can have all sorts of meanings, like the imagery of our dreams. Things can, of course, come to pass on a variety of levels. Some say what is resolved on a mental level does not have to manifest materially.

While compiling this chapter it has not been possible to explore each body of prophecy as it deserves, for that would amount to many volumes. However, it is worth bearing in mind that not everything is always quite as it seems and even the most earnest reporters and interpreters can make mistakes. For many facts we can only rely on the words of others and authors who have obviously been at pains to research their material still get it wrong. My speciality is astrology and, as an example, I have seen cases where clear distinction is not made between the tropical and sidereal zodiacs (i.e. the zodiac by the season and the zodiac by the stars) in predictions. In addition, there have been places where planetary positions have been quoted for a certain time, that are quite wrong, as a glance at planetary tables will confirm. This is not an invitation to disregard the whole shebang. The smoke signals say that something is happening. However, it is a reminder to keep things in perspective.

During the process of reviewing current prophecies, I have moved through unease into hope. Interpretations of prophecies in the 1960s and 1970s were generally apocalyptic. However, as some things have not come to pass (although, of course, they still may) the climate has become more positive and there is talk of a rise in consciousness and the evolution of humanity. It is true, I feel, that we are learning. Not perhaps in sufficient numbers, as yet, but the shift is beginning. The teaching of the Native Americans and other indigenous people worldwide is gradually finding its way into the mainstream as the dross is rubbed off the ancient wisdom, letting its pure gold shine through. The message to respect the earth is getting louder and we are trying to find new ways, to discover what is really of value in ourselves and to love it as we love our neighbour. Hopi prophecy tells of cycles. First was the cycle of the mineral, then came that of the plant and then the cycle of the animal. Now we are coming to the end of the animal cycle and we have investigated ourselves, learning what it is like to be an animal on this earth. We stand now on the threshold of the cycle of the human being, when our greatest powers are about to be discovered. Open the box!

5 THE MAYA – MYSTERY AND PROPHECY

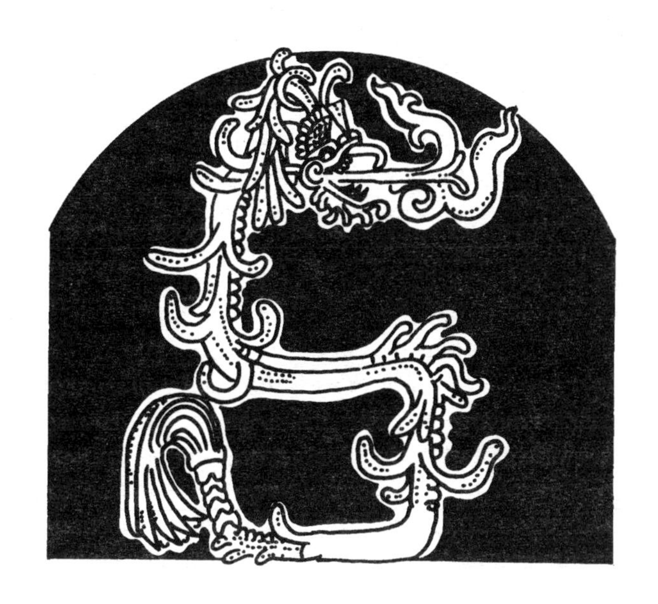

Art is long, and Time is fleeting
And our hearts, though stout and brave
Still, like muffled drums, are beating
Funeral marches to the grave.

H.W. LONGFELLOW, *A PSALM OF LIFE*

Lost civilisations possess an enduring fascination. Aside from pure curiosity – who were they?; how did they disappear? – there lurks the idea that they may have known a thing or two that we do not, or that we may have forgotten. We are aware that, as a culture and as individuals, we are not operating at full throttle; it is well known that only one-tenth of the brain is used. At the same time incidents of extrasensory perception (ESP) hint at extra powers that could be developed. However, our linear concept of time, our arrogance regarding our science and its achievements and the conviction (which is, actually, hardly logical) that latest, most modern is bound to equal most advanced, means that we approach investigation of lost cultures hampered by preconceptions. Several things may need to be borne in mind. First, the most advanced cultures do not necessarily leave the most noticeable traces (even if we equate 'advancement' with the type of consumerism and materialism with which we are familiar). For example, a satellite in space off which to bounce radio signals may mean no telegraph poles left for future generations to discover, and thus it may be assumed that the civilisation in question did not possess the telephone. Second, it is always possible that the civilisation under investigation was so far in advance of our current understanding that we are simply unable to comprehend the traces – imagine a medieval peasant's thoughts on finding the remains of a television set. Third, we need to take off our blinkers, which is not always easy, as we are not quite sure what and where they are. We need to attempt to approach the clues with a mind as free from twentieth-century conditioning as possible. As we enter the new millennium, one of the most important messages such 'lost' cultures may have for us is how and why they met their end, for this may suggest to us the dangers we face and how we may deal with them.

HISTORY AND ORIGINS OF THE MAYA

One of the most fascinating and least understood lost cultures is that of the Maya, who emerged from the mists around 2000 BCE and dissolved back into them mysteriously, around 800 CE, leaving only their post-classic stragglers. Their remnants are tangled in the jungles of Central America where their most famous city, Palenque, was discovered in 1773, since when their enigma has teased historians and writers. Palenque has still not been fully investigated and the walls of its pyramids and temples contain many inscriptions that we are only beginning to decipher. The Maya did not use the wheel and their ability to move 30-tonne blocks of stone is one of many mysteries.

It seems that Mayan life was simple with a society based on a hierarchical caste system, in which the peasants tilled the land while the rulers undertook strenuous rituals. However, this culture was not by any means ignorant, for Mayan traces display a highly sophisticated knowledge of astronomy with an extremely complex calender. The meanings of this calendrical system have profound implications for us and possibly for our very survival. Although the Maya lived without anything we would regard as a basic modern convenience, it may well be that their psychic faculties were highly developed. Like many indigenous peoples they actively used dreams as a means of prognosis and for deeper understanding. Mayans may have used some of their buildings for 'temple sleep' in which revelation was sought for knowledge or healing. It seems also that the Mayans had the concept of totem or power animals, similar to that which is familiar in Native North American culture, suggesting a shamanic element in their society (i.e. they may have believed in 'spirit flight' practised by magical priests, whose wisdom would have guided the populace).

Believing that salvation was possible only through mortification of the flesh, the Maya underwent painful rituals, such as piercing the penis with a ceremonial lance, and bloodletting. The Mayans also practised flattening the foreheads of babies born to the nobility, which was extremely painful and not infrequently resulted in death.

Conventional anthropology describes this merely as a fashion fad, but this must surely be unlikely. Another idea is that it may have enabled the brain to function more effectively, contributing to the highly developed spatial skills of the Maya. One of the remains discovered at Palenque consists of strange objects similar to flowers placed upon a skull and it is quite possible that these were magnetic in nature, designed to impinge upon the central locus of the pineal/hypothalamus area of the brain and so bring the functions of the brain hemispheres into tandem. In practice, this could have meant that the Maya, or at least those who had undergone this treatment, could have access to their 'right brain' instinctual and pattern-perceiving faculties, able to marry these with the logical, linear thinking of the left brain, possibly to enhance their consciousness in ways that may have given them greatly expanded abilities.

The earliest origins of these people are indistinct. Archaeologists believe that the Maya and other ancient tribes of America came from Asia, traversing the land bridge that used to be where the Bering Strait is now found, about 30,000 years ago. However, Edgar Cayce and others have suggested that they may have been survivors of a cataclysm that brought about the destruction of Atlantis. Stories about Atlantis have flourished for many years to the point where it has become a cliché and a subject of derision among scholars. However, Plato in *Critias* and *Timaeus* is quite clear that there was once a land mass beyond the Pillars of Hercules (i.e. Gibraltar) and that Athenians were descendants of some of the survivors of the 'deluge' that destroyed this continent. Cayce further indicated that the records of the Atlantean civilisation were of 'One' civilisation but divided between three places, namely Egypt, the Bimini area of the Caribbean and the Yucatan, and that these repositories would come to light by 1998, when the consciousness of humankind had risen to the required level. An ancient Mayan document, called the Codex Tro-Cortesianus, mentions a great catastrophe that befell

Central America in the remote past, and an oral tradition regarding the destruction of a great civilisation in the Atlantic Ocean was catalogued by Charles Etienne Brasseur de Bourbourg, a Mayan scholar of the nineteenth century. Bourbourg also speculated that the ancient civilisations of South America and Egypt could have originated with Atlantis. Mayan records speak of Five Ages of civilisation, each of which is followed by a cataclysm. The end of the first age would correspond to about 10,500 BCE and the end of Atlantis, the speculation being that survivors sailed west, possibly in advance of the anticipated catastrophe, founding the later Mayan culture. Of this we cannot be sure, but there is surely no reason why this should not be the case. No conclusive evidence has been uncovered that confirms or denies the hypothesis.

There have always been scholars who believe that the Mayan skill in pyramid building was imported. A story exists of a traveller called Votan, whose symbol was the serpent and who came from the east with followers wearing robes, helping to found the city of Palenque. Votan came from Valum Chivim which has been identified as Tripoli. Many scholars are highly sceptical about this and other tales. However, certain depictions upon Mayan remains show faces that appear Middle Eastern, and there have been many pieces of evidence pointing to pre-Columbian expeditions to the Americas. Thor Heyerdahl in his boat *Ra II* proved that it would certainly have been possible for the Egyptians to cross the Atlantic. However, if we postulate the existence of some older civilisation, Egyptians themselves would hardly have needed to make the journey for parallels to exist between the cultures. Indeed, there exist many parallels between the astronomy and cosmology of the Mayans and Egyptians. It is possible that both civilisations shared a common ancestry in Atlantis, or elsewhere. On this and other questions the jury is still out.

The Lid of Palenque

THE LID OF PALENQUE

Of all the artefacts unearthed in relation to the Maya the Lid of Palenque is the most interesting and the most revealing. This lid covered a tomb found within the Temple of Inscriptions in Palenque. Weighing 5 tonnes it is too large to be removed and remains still within the sarcophagus. The tomb is the last resting place of the Lord Pacal, who was a most respected king, dying at the age of 80 in 683 CE. In *Chariots of the Gods* Erich von Daniken speculated that the figure on the centre of the Lid of Palenque was a spaceman at the controls of his craft, and while the idea of prehistoric alien visitors responsible for the genesis of civilisation was popular in the 1960s and 1970s these have now largely been discredited on the grounds of insufficient evidence. None the less, von Daniken's books continue to sell and to be reprinted and reissued. A more likely identification of the central figure is the goddess Chalchiuhtlicue, who presided over the first of the Five Ages of humankind, in which the Maya believed. Representatives of three other ages are discernible, but that of our own current era, the jaguar, could not at first be located.

What is of interest here is less whether or not we owe much in our past to visitors from outer space, than the remarkable properties of the Lid of Palenque. The lid has a border of symbols that relate to the Five Ages and the types of destruction that followed them, but one of the most puzzling features of the lid is the fact that two of its corners have been broken, or chiselled off, cutting into the design and rendering it incomplete. It is inconceivable that this could have been accidental, so why was this deliberately done to an artefact over which endless trouble had been taken?

The Maya believed that each individual was a piece of Creation, and that all things became at some point their opposite. Thus, day becomes night, summer becomes winter, I am you and you are me and what is absent is, in fact, subtly present and emphasised, in a universe of complementary dualities. In a brilliant piece of lateral thinking, the engineer and writer Maurice Cotterell applied this philosophy to the missing corners of the lid, wondering if, in fact, they were not 'missing' at all. By making acetate copies of the engravings and laying them one on top of the other the full pattern reappeared and many other engravings made sense, in terms of Mayan mythology and solar cycles, even suggesting the loops of magnetism on the sun that give rise to sunspots. By keying together the five-dot central border code from the lid, in acetate overlays, the jaguar symbol of our own, Fifth Age was revealed. These interpretations were rejected by experts on the basis that the Maya did not have acetates! However, the power of visualisation and the necessity to be able to do this clearly and in detail is stressed by many wisdom teachings. In fact, the ability to envision and to memorise is something that has certainly declined in us since writing became available to all, and even more so since the advent of television. It seems highly likely that the Mayan powers of memory and visualisation were far in advance of anything we possess today, and suggests that the messages on the lid were intended for those who had the skill to decipher them.

QUETZALCOATL

The snake and the eagle are creatures of potent symbology, found in many mythologies. Both are associated with the astrological sign Scorpio and, while this may seem of slender relevance for most individuals born with the sun in Scorpio, the point is that the theme of destruction and regeneration that is associated with the sign is embodied by these beasts. The connection of the serpent with the earth, on which it crawls, is obvious. Snakes represent our instinctual, basic natures and they also hint at the mysteries of cycle and manifestation by their spiralling movements – the snake speaks of primal wisdom and also of subtle energies, for the kundalini energies that can raise consciousness are portrayed as coiled at the base of the spine. The soaring eagle is symbolic of transcendence and exaltation. Both of these images, along with that of the phoenix, magical bird that rises renewed from its funeral pyre, come together in the image of Quetzalcoatl, the plumed serpent and the saviour god of the Maya and other Central American peoples, such as the Aztecs. Quetzalcoatl can be seen as one of a legion of dying and resurrecting saviour gods, representational of the seasonal cycle and the ever-renewing promise of Nature, and so he is connected to the sun, which 'dies' and resurrects.

The serpent was very important to the Maya, in particular the rattlesnake, a subspecies of *Crotalus durissus durissus* which the Maya called Ahau Can or 'Great lordly serpent'. The biological cycles of this snake fit closely with important times in the calendar, for it sheds its skin when the sun over the Yucatan peninsula reaches its highest point for the second time in the year, while it sheds and replaces its fangs every 20 days, which was a unit of time called a *uinal* and important to the Maya. In addition, the pattern of rectangles on the skin of the snake was reproduced in the plan of buildings that were orientated to the four cardinal points. The symbolism of the snake was pervasive among the Maya and the flattened heads adopted by dangerous ordeal caused the head to resemble that of a serpent. The whole idea of this snake-dominated culture and symbolism is in a way similar to the cross in Christian parts of the world, and I suspect that we have not yet got to the bottom of the true significance.

The stories of Quetzalcoatl, who, in one story, immolated himself upon a pyre from which rare birds arose, are most complex, combining god and man. Quetzalcoatl goes by many names, including those of Zapotec, Kukulcan and Kon Tiki. He has been shown tall, with fair skin and European features, tattooed with the figures of unknown animals, that some have interpreted as an indication that he was a prehistoric hero/invader/spiritual leader, either from Europe or a lost continent. Legend states that he came from the south after a catastrophe that had hidden the sun, so he 'brought back the sun' as a solar god/hero would, but also as the survivor of the same disaster would have done. The cultural myths of Quetzalcoatl underlay the calendrical measurements of the Maya and other Mesoamerican peoples, for Quetzalcoatl was a god, a mythical archetype, a human ruler, a high priest and a hero. He was identified with Venus, the Morning and Evening star, which the Maya, unlike many early cultures, understood were one and the same celestial body. Linked also to fertility and the springs of life, Quetzalcoatl was the germinating power within the seed, lord of healing and magic, infused with learning and clothed in beauty. He also meant transcendent, cosmic intelligence. The quetzal bird, with its bright plumage, was considered the most strikingly lovely of birds, while *coatl* means serpent. Mayan art is full of human heads emerging from the jaws of a serpent, symbolising enlightenment as the kundalini power energises the chakras and brings about cosmic consciousness. Quetzalcoatl thus represented the highest human potential – that to which we aspire in this 'New Age'. Like many such figures, his meaning only grows in power in our time.

Coatl, in Aztec, also mans 'twin' and Quetzalcoatl had a dark counterpart called Tezcatlipoca, who brought trouble to the paradisical world ruled by the enlightened one. Quetzalcoatl has much in common with heroes such as King Arthur who are brought low by a relative (in Arthur's case his illegitimate son, Mordred). This really is a manifestation of the shadow, which we discuss in Chapter 8. Encounter with the shadow is the basis for evolution, in myth, in the human personality and as may soon become apparent, globally. The incorporation of the shadow, or repressed elements, is a vital step in the reclamation of potential for true knowledge and progress. For all his glory, the original Quetzalcoatl had not made peace with this aspect – he was rather too good to be true! Quetzalcoatl is thus brought low by his dark twin. Extraneously, the glory of Mesoamerica fell and the transcendent practice of opening the heart chakra was replaced by a literal fundamentalism that resulted in hearts being torn out and sacrificed to the sun god. In the story of Quetzalcoatl, following his fall, the god-king now departed, prophesying his return to claim his kingdom in the future. It was said that if he returned on the Mayan date 1-Reed kings would be struck down.

On just that date the conquistador Cortes landed in 1519. This was the designated start of the Nine Hells of the Mayan calendar. Because of the prophecy the Aztecs, heirs to the Maya, did not fully resist invasion. Their ruler, Montezuma, was murdered and the empire destroyed. During the first 'Hell' of 52 years, an estimated population of 25 million people in Mesoamerica was reduced to only 1 million. The only good thing that one can say about this is that it was a type of purification of what had become a debased and cruel culture and, in a sense, it was indeed the return of Quetzalcoatl, or rather Tezcatlipoca, the vengeful aspect of the god.

This story is interesting for its many layers of meaning, its complex symbols and its indication that prophecy, when it is fulfilled, does not always come quite as we expect. For us, entering the third millennium, such symbols are also most important. Stories of King Arthur, for instance, the 'once and future king' become ever more popular, as we sense

the need for a hero, a unifying figure. Some interpret the return of Arthur as a unification of male and female principles, the King as the Masculine principle and the light of consciousness defending the Land as Feminine principle, root of life and the instinctual domain. Similar meanings can be discerned in the Mayan myth, as the enlightened consciousness grows from instinctual wells (i.e. the head emerging from the serpent, the motif of the 'plumed serpent' itself). The true 'return of Quetzalcoatl' may be seen as enlightenment, or a Christ-consciousness.

The rebirth into a new consciousness depicted by the phoenix story and the many symbolic meanings of serpent and eagle thus applies for us. What does the serpent suggest of our true origins? What does the eagle indicate about our potentials? By this, I mean, among other things, that we have yet truly to discover what are the energies that constitute life, as represented by the serpent, and what we are actually developing towards, as represented by the eagle. Perhaps the Maya had a better idea. Because of some occurrence, the nature of which is still not known, their civilisation collapsed in the early centuries of the second millennium, but they have left us plenty of messages that are connected to their measurements of time and the complexities of their calender.

THE MAYAN CALENDAR

Priceless wisdom, possibly from the dawn of humankind, has been lost in the conquest of Meso-America. Small wonder that the Mayans wailed as the bishops consigned their great fan-folded books to the flames, as evidence of devil worship! The Maya were apparently obsessed with numbers, which many philosophers have considered the basis of creation, and they computed time and cycles in ways that can seem complex. However, if you do not share this love of numbers you may like to skim over some of the following passages! The complexities of the Mayan calendar contain valuable secrets that are beginning now to be revealed. During the nineteenth century, the writer and cleric, Charles Etienne Brasseur de Bourbourg was able to clarify some of the elements of Mayan time-keeping, demonstrating that, far from being ignorant savages, the Maya were highly sophisticated.

Both the Aztecs and the Maya used two calendars. First, there was the repeating cycle of 260 days, called a *tzolkin*; second, there was the 'vague year' of *haab* of 365 days, used for agriculture and practical purposes. However, this wasn't so 'vague' for it was calculated as 365.242129 days and was probably more accurate than our own Gregorian calendar of 365.2425 days. The tzolkin cycle was sacred and ceremonial and is still used for magical purposes to this day by remote Mayan tribes still extant. The tzolkin is based on the counting together of 20 day names with the numbers 1 to 13. This is not done in sequence, as we do, but more after the manner of 1 January, 2 February, 3 March and so forth. Each of the 20 day names had a unique and symbolic meaning – for instance, the world was said to have been originally created on the back of an alligator; thus the calendar was said to have begun originally on 1 Alligator. 'Reed' synchronised cycles and marked new beginnings, and after the Spanish conquest the calendar was changed to begin with this glyph. 'Flower' is the last glyph, because the end of the creation process is beauty. The two cycles, haab and tzolkin, coincided every 52 years, called the Aztec Century, and some sources say that the haab was brought in line with actual solar cycles by a 13-day adjustment, every 52 years, instead of our system of Leap Years. Mayan cosmology depicted 13 heaven and 9 hell realms, and the calendar corresponded with this, for 13 of the 52-year cycles made a cycle of Thirteen Heavens (676 years) followed by a Nine Hells cycle of 9×52 (468 years). As we saw, the Nine Hells

cycle started with the arrival of Cortes in 1519. It ended in 1987, date of the Harmonic Convergence and the Blue Star supernova, encountered in Chapter 4.

Haab and tzolkin were fine for short periods of time, but for longer time periods they had obvious limitations so the Maya had, in addition, a calendar called the Long Count. As part of this, individual days were counted, as follows:

- 20 days = 1 uinal (20-day 'month')
- 18 uinals = 1 tun (360-day 'year')
- 20 tuns = 1 katun (7,200 days)
- 20 katuns = 1 baktun (144,000 days).

For many years it was impossible to align these dates with the Gregorian calendar, and so the Mayan calendar was unanchored, until earlier in the twentieth century when the esteemed Mayanologist Eric Thompson identified the start of the present Mayan Great Cycle as 13 August, 3114 BCE. Such a cycle lasts for 13 baktuns (i.e. 1,872,999 days), which is 5,125.40 years and amounts to one-fifth of the exact Maya reckoning of the Precession of the Equinoxes – 25,627 years. The end of the present age will arrive on 22 December, 2012.

The layout of Mayan architecture, in terms of orientation of buildings and site of roof-combs, reveals that their astronomical knowledge was sound and very sophisticated, marking the movements of the constellations, especially the Pleiades, the planets and of eclipses. The cycle of the planet Venus was of especial interest, and this planet was called the Quetzalcoatl star. The current Great Cycle began with an event called The Birth of Venus, when Venus rose just before dawn with the Pleiades at the meridian. On 22 December, 2012, Venus 'dies' going down just before the sun, as the Pleiades rises over the eastern horizon. This can be seen as the start of a new precessional cycle and world age, and it coincides with the Mayan prediction for the end of the last of the Five Ages. The extreme complexity of Mayan mathematics and astronomy are interwoven with metaphysics and mythology in such a way that it has been described as a possible shorthand for a type of galactic science that goes beyond our present physics and extends into other dimensions. The Maya may have had a galactic masterplan of majestic dimensions that we are only just beginning to glimpse. They may also have possessed scientific knowledge about our sun that is highly relevant for us.

Another number emerges that is of paramount importance, identified in a Mayan document called the Dresden Codex. The number is 1,366,560, and it is composed of numbers of days in several ways:

- 260 × 5,256 (number of tzolkins)
- 365 × 3,744 (number of vague years)
- 584 × 2,340 (number of average cycles of the planet Venus)
- 78 × 1,752 (number of Mars cycles)
- 18,980 × 72 (number of Aztec centuries, i.e. 73 tzolkins/52 vague years)

There seemed little sense to the system of baktuns, katuns, etc. until the writer Maurice Cotterell, employing the same approach that had yielded success with the Lid of Palenque, realised that the key lay in what was missing (i.e. the all-important 260-day interval). Using the Mayan esoteric number 9, the following pattern emerges:

144,000 (baktun)	×	9 =	1,296,000
7,200 (katun)	×	9 =	64,800
360 (tun)	×	9 =	3,240
260 (tzolkin)	×	9 =	2,340
20 (uinal)	×	9 =	180
		Total	**1,366,560**

The above system, upon examination, appears complex, but it reflects a highly developed knowledge of important cycles within cycles that modern techniques are now revealing and corroborating, as we shall discover.

ASTROLOGY, SUNSPOTS AND THE FUTURE OF LIFE

Mayan use of astrological ideas is evident from their buildings and surviving texts. This is no surprise, for many ancient civilisations used knowledge of the stars and planets as significators for their lives. Today astrology is largely frowned upon by the scientific establishment, but it continues to fascinate the man and woman in the street and engages the minds of some fine and subtle thinkers. Is it likely that something so enduring is of no significance? Many astrologers will assert that whatever the explanation, or non-explanation, behind the art/science may be, their astrology is based upon observation, and it works. It was this attitude of observation that engaged Maurice Cotterell, when he noticed that men born under Fire signs (Aries, Leo, Sagittarius) tended to be more aggressive than their colleagues, born under one of the other nine signs. Although the astrological signs are named after constellations, because of a movement called 'precession' where the earth wobbles on its axis, the signs and constellations no longer coincide, thus it is the time of year that is of greatest importance.

Looking for a cause for this, Cotterell decided to investigate sunspots. These are areas of relative coolness on the surface of the sun and their frequency seems to follow a cycle of some 11 years. Sunspots are thought to be caused by 'loops' of magnetism upon the sun, created by the variable rotation of the surface of the sun and its complex magnetic field. The sun is not a solid body but a ball of plasma gas, rotating more slowly at its poles than at the equator. In addition, the magnetic field of the sun is dipolar at the poles and quadripolar at the equator. The sun throws off a constant stream of negative or positively charged particles, called the solar wind, and this gives rise to the phenomenon of the Aurora Borealis. Maurice Cotterell gathered evidence for his theory that it was the cyclic variation in the solar wind, affecting the earth's gravitational field that caused astrological effects, although these effects were operative at conception, rather than birth. The scientific establishment ignored his findings, and it is to the credit of astrologers that he was at least given 10 minutes to speak at an International Conference hosted by the British Astrological Society, even though his research threatened the basis of most modern astrology (i.e. the significance of the time of birth, not conception).

Cotterell's later work did, in fact, progress to suggest that time of birth is significant, for the foetus reacts to conditions created by the solar wind, relative to those operative at time of conception, to release the hormones that trigger birth. The effect upon human genetics of sunspots and the solar wind had received attention, but Maurice Cotterell was engaged upon further investigations concerning solar effects. He found that there was an 11.49-year cycle for sunspot activity, but also that there were longer cycles concerning the angles between the magnetic fields of the earth and the sun. Every 87.4545 days the sun's equatorial and polar fields complete a 'cycle' and come back to zero point. A period of eight of these cycles formed another cycle, which he called a 'microcycle' and, in turn, six microcycles made up a cycle of 11.49299 years. A longer period emerged of 187 years, made up of 97 microcycles, but whereas each of these microcycles might have been expected to have been made up from eight of the smallest cycles, as mentioned above, in fact five of them were made up of an extra cycle, making 781 of the original 87.4545-day rotational periods, not 776. Closer

investigation revealed that this anomaly was caused by the warped shape of the neutral sheet encircling the sun's equator. Like all magnets, the polar field of the sun has an area of balance, or neutrality but, because of the complexity of the sun's structure, this area is kinked. The cycle of this neutral sheet takes a total of 97×187-year cycles, that is 18,139 years.

The most interesting fact about the latter statistic is that it can be broken down into five ages, which correspond with alterations in the polarity of the sun's magnetic field and the movement of the warped neutral sheet, as follows:

- 1,297,738 days (19 × 187 years)
- 1,366,040 days (20 × 187 years)
- 1,297,738 days (19 × 187 years)
- 1,297,738 days (19 × 187 years)
- 1,366,040 days (20 × 187 years)

These five cycles of time and magnetic interaction seem to correspond with the five ages of the Maya. The number 1,366,040 seems too similar to the Mayan special number 1,366,560 to be a coincidence, especially as the difference between the two numbers corresponds to two of the Mayan tzolkins of 260 days each (i.e. 520 days). At the end of each of the timespans the sun's magnetic field shifts, causing changes also in the magnetic field of the earth and consequent climatic and seismic upheaval. The interval of 13 baktuns (i.e. 1,872,000 days) mentioned above is also significant for, although it contains an incomplete number of sunspot cycles, it relates to a longer cycle and does, in fact, draw attention, by mathematical process, to the cycle of precession (i.e. the 'wobble' of the earth on its axis and the cycle of the warped neutral sheet of the sun, which affects the magnetic climate). Could it be that the 'primitive' Maya, who did not even use the wheel, knew possibly more than we do about the solar fluctuations and their effect upon life on earth?

ANCIENT KNOWLEDGE AND ARMAGGEDON

Periods of low sunspot activity tend to mark times of cultural decline, seemingly linked to the effect that solar activity has upon human fertility. There is considerable evidence to suggest that the Maya anticipated their decline in the seventh century CE. The cycles of Venus were used to monitor sunspot cycles. The Mayan Long Count started with the Birth of Venus, 12 August 3114 BCE. The full cycle, tracked by the movement of Venus, comes to the number 1,366,560 as mentioned above, and this reaches completion at the time of Mayan disappearance, when sunspot activity was low and solar magnetic shift was at its centre. Solar magnetic changes may affect the earth's magnetosphere, thus allowing greater penetration by cosmic rays which would be felt more keenly in equatorial regions. Not only the shifting phase of the solar neutral sheet but also the changing polarity of the sunspot cycle affects human fertility, and this latter factor is operative at the moment, perhaps causing more infertility than pollution and other matters. In addition, we are already experiencing climatic changes and, while these may be due to global warming, they might also be a foretaste of the destruction in 2012 believed by some to be foretold by the Maya. Although the sun is giver of warmth and life, it can also deal death. No doubt a fear of solar power was behind the unpleasant habit of the Aztecs, successors to the Maya, of sacrificing many thousands of people to the sun, by ripping the still-beating heart out of the chest of the victim, to placate the sun's voracious appetite.

Mayan lore gives accounts of the destruction of the world at the end of the former four periods, by water, wind and fire. Certainly it is known that the magnetic field of the earth has shifted before, which may explain the disappearance of the dinosaurs. If the earth were to tilt on its axis, massive earthquakes would shake the globe, the atmosphere and the oceans would continue to move in the usual fashion, due to inertia, thus giving rise to massive tidal waves and hurricanes of unimaginable ferocity. Lava would spew out over large areas, mountains would be swallowed and lands rise up from the depths of the ocean, as Atlantis is predicted to 'rise again'. From combined studies of Mayan timekeeping and sunspot activity, Maurice Cotterell believes that the prophecy for the end of the fifth age concerns a reversal of the magnetic field of the earth, because of shifts in the magnetic pattern of the sun and the cycle of the warped neutral sheet. This cataclysm is due to occur in or around 2012. The complete account is given in *The Maya Prophecies* by Maurice Cotterell and Adrian Gilbert (see Further Reading).

CONCLUSION

Are we to expect the destruction of our civilisation and most of life currently existing upon earth, early in the twenty-first century? Our brief lives are little more than an eye-blink relative to the cycles of earth and sun so we have the illusion that our world and its rhythms are solid and unchanging. From a cosmic viewpoint they are about as stable as a conker dangling on the end of a string. However, there exist differing approaches to interpretation of Mayan records, and we have by no means fully understood the scope of the Mayan vision. Statistics can be in error and misinterpretation is always possible. Cortes would have found the conquest of Central America much more difficult, even impossible had he not had the awesome mantle of Quetzalcoatl erroneously thrust upon him, because of a prophecy. The Maya themselves appear to have held a fatalistic attitude, which may conceivably have been a race memory of an earlier cataclysm and, despite their knowledge, they do not appear to have been able or perhaps motivated to prevent their own demise.

None the less, there are lessons to be learnt from the Mayan prophecies. One of these is surely that we should approach ancient records and relics in a spirit of some humility. Despite our technology we may be dealing with remnants of civilisations that are far in advance of our own and there is no reason why this should not be so. Also, bearing in mind that global destruction is always undeniably possible, from reversals in magnetic field to collision with comets or meteorites, what on earth are we doing using our developing knowledge to make more devices of mass destruction with which to terrorise each other, when we should be using it to evolve survival plans? The twenty-first century is a call for a global consciousness, to unite our efforts, to have a respect for our species and a determination to preserve it. It seems to amount almost to this; that we will succeed in preserving ourselves only if we merit being preserved. The price of survival may be co-operation.

The final word here has to go to the Maya legends themselves, which also seem to indicate a golden future that has images in common with the latter part of the book of Revelation. This is extracted from Tony Shearer's *Lord of the Dawn* (Happy Camp, CA: Naturegraph, 1971)

> *Thirteen Heavens of decreasing choice,*
> *Nine Hells of increasing doom,*
> *and the Tree of Life shall blossom with a fruit*
> *never before known in creation.*
> *And that fruit shall be the New Spirit of Man.*

6 THE 'NEW AGE'

Perhaps the characteristic that makes us most human is our capacity to do the unnatural, to transcend and hence transform our own nature.

M. SCOTT PECK, *THE ROAD LESS TRAVELLED*

WHAT IS THE NEW AGE?

In reaction to our spiritually bereft, consumer-orientated society, a considerable counter-culture has evolved and is especially noticeable at the end of the 1990s. Sometimes this has been little more than cosmetic, amounting to a few moons and stars and crystals, but in many cases it extends along a spectrum of taste and awareness into a total lifestyle and belief system. Many readers will no doubt be part of this movement in some form. For those of you who find it all rather confusing, let us delve beneath the surface of this alternative scene.

The interesting points about what is often referred to as the 'New Age' (a catch-all term to which many people object, but which still serves to set the scene) is that it has so many different strands and that it is increasingly influential upon the mainstream. Many people find that old methods no longer serve them or that the system has let them down; relationships fail, jobs disappear and health breaks down. Solutions, or a least fresh thoughts about such problems, are usually to be found somewhere in the 'New Age' scene. Individuals and established disciplines are turning increasingly to alternative solutions and there is growing cross-fertilisation and tolerance. The New Age is not something that has to be accepted or rejected *en masse* and most people are finding something to interest or to help them under its umbrella. As we enter the twenty-first century I think we can expect more of the alternative scene to become generally accepted and welcomed, with the wheat separated from the chaff and combined with more conventional approaches which will themselves be modified in the light of more imaginative but workable perspectives.

HUMAN POTENTIAL

One of the most noticeable movements is that of 'Human Potential' founded to some extent by Fritz Perls, a Gestalt therapist. All forms of psychotherapy, from depth analysis to supportive work, are truly a phenomenon of the twentieth century. Increasingly, problems are responded to by a wish to understand the dynamics at work, especially in oneself.

We are aware of our power as individuals and no longer necessarily accept the voice of one authority or another, and we want to know what 'makes us tick'. Roles are changing and the old securities are disappearing in an unprecedented manner and speed. Forms of counselling and therapy are sought in order to help us to improve our condition and to deepen self-awareness. They are also a means by which we can grab some feeling of control, when all seems to be out of control. Therapy can also help us to develop our potential, to be the 'best possible me' and to be the architects of our own lives, thinking 'positive thoughts' and enhancing our self-esteem, our integration as individuals and our communicative skills. The growth in the popularity of many forms of counselling is also a response to the isolation of modern life and the absence of the village 'wise-woman' or 'cunning man' or similar. In the twenty-first century I suspect that the ideas within counselling and similar forms of therapy will become more popular, although possibly in an altering format as millenarian hysteria recedes, with more knowledge of what can and cannot be achieved, with a social context taking the place of some of the preoccupation with self. A spiritual dimension may emerge more specifically, with increased 'self-help' as the ideas offered by counsellors become generally understood and modified as part of the evolving culture.

It has also been argued that the boom in counselling is due to a large extent to millenarian anxiety, manifesting as problems in relationships or jobs but due, in truth, to a profound unease regarding the huge changes that face us. This may be a response to social shifts, or it may be a fear produced simply by the number 2,000. None of us really welcomes what is unfamiliar. We carry a universal angst in the face of the unpredictability of life and we are capable of becoming a little alarmed simply by our own counting system!

Another drive that may be discerned tends towards holistic or 'positive' health. This is underpinned by several strands of thought. A belief is growing that we create our own health or lack of it by our lifestyle and by our thoughts, that we can be healthy if we learn how to let go of bad feelings, work through our problems instead of denying they exist and generally 'think healthy'. The holistic outlook perceives mind and body as a unit and physical health as dependent to a great extent upon the mind. Indeed, the holistic concept extends far beyond this and can be seen as one of the factors behind astrology and similar subjects, with the individual and the universe conceived as an interconnected whole. In the case of bodily ailments, these may be a metaphor for psychological problems – for instance, the person who suffers from continual throat troubles may never be saying what needs to be said, in order to express feelings and needs, and so the body flags up the problem in the shape of laryngitis or a similar ailment. Health can be seen as a 'positive' state of vibrant well-being rather than the absence of disease. Interventionist and invasive methods are questioned because they attack the disease instead of strengthening the body – disease itself may be seen as a symptom of underlying imbalance and the alternative approach is to ask what continual infections, or even cancer, 'mean' in the context of life. The idea here may be that if one can define where one is going wrong one can put it right and the disease will disappear. Sometimes this works dramatically; at others it is sadly akin to 'blaming the victim' and it can be applied in a manner that is far too simplistic. None the less, the link between mental state and physical health is increasingly accepted by established medicine.

LIFESTYLES AND INTERESTS

Renewed respect for our bodies and the wish to take care of them and really to think about how we are treating them, as well as an enhanced sense of responsibility for ourselves and the impact we have on our environment, has led to a vast increase in vegetarianism, yoga and similar disciplines, exercise classes of varying sorts (which can hardly be called 'alternative') and massage. As chemical additives, modern farming methods and genetic engineering control more and more of what we eat, concern is growing regarding the ethics of these methods and their possible unknown dangers, and many people are examining their habits, choosing natural foodstuffs produced in a humane, sustainable and often organic manner. Instead of pills and antibiotics, forms of therapy which promote the body's own healing abilities are continually growing in popularity, such as aromatherapy, reflexology, acupuncture, herbalism, homoeopathy, to name but a few. This comes also in response to the realisation of the drawbacks and limitations in conventional medicine. Again, there is the drive to be the 'best possible me' and/or to be responsible for one's own health and, therefore, in control. There is also the issue of being a responsible 'global citizen'.

Other aspects to the 'New Age' include a general interest in the occult. This covers an immense sweep, from fortune telling to UFOs. 'Energies' is the buzz term, for what may be sensed at special places on the earth or indeed for anything that may be apprehended by senses other than our usual five. This is something of a cliché, regarded with scepticism by many people. However, while there is no doubt some self-deception and pretence, something, or things, are definitely being sensed by people who then have to struggle with the limitations of our language in order to express themselves. Thus 'energies' covers a wide spectrum of the 'becoming known'. The underlying drives in occult interests seem to be to examine all possibilities and to dismiss nothing merely on the basis that it does not fit into the accepted patterns and received wisdom, a wish to understand dimensions of experience not formerly navigated and also a wish to expand our own abilities. Some people believe that we are all becoming more 'psychic' as the next step in our evolution. We are looking for 'something more' and may be willing to countenance almost anything as the old taboos lose their meaning. Possibly we have paranormal skills and are capable of experiences that have been hitherto beyond the imagination. (The increase in 'channelling' which is, broadly speaking, a type of mediumship, where messages from the higher planes or beings that inhabit them are channelled through someone who is sensitive, is one example.) To a greater or lesser extent, such thoughts may be entertained by those exploring the alternative scene. Studies of the paranormal and related subjects may be extra-attractive because they were proscribed until comparatively recently. In addition, many of the esoteric arts, such as astrology or tarot, offer us avenues to know ourselves better and/or to know the future. In an uncertain environment, such sources are increasingly magnetic.

One response to the threats of our modern condition and the aggression and competition that is rife has been a rather undefined movement towards 'universal love', peace and light, characterised by dolphins, rainbows and similar symbols. This is often pleasant, indeed beautiful, but may fail to address certain conflicts and problems of an inner nature, and so be little more than cosmetic. Energy vortices, earth chakras and places of power may be sought more in the spirit of the consumer than the pilgrim. Former incarnations (usually as someone notable or charismatic, such as Cleopatra or a Lakota shaman) may be explored, auras cleansed and magical sigils dangled from every limb. This has been satirised, and it is true that there is much that is delusory, hypocritical and plain 'kooky' about the New Age. None the less, the entire movement should not be dismissed as self-deception and fashion fad, for there is much more at work here.

One reaction to our synthetic and de-spiritualised environment has been a growth in interest in ethnic and ancient wisdom-teachings, such as that of the Native Americans and Tibetans. We feel we have become alienated from part of ourselves, from our heritage, from the earth and from perceptions that were once our birthright. Many seekers are exploring ways to reinstate native traditions and to rediscover something within themselves. This extends from fostering a respect for the earth and a value in the simple ways, through to the growth in the practice of shamanism itself, which is the art of 'spirit flight' central to most, if not all 'primitive' societies. In contrast to channelling, shamanism is a purposeful trance, usually entered into on the background of a drumbeat. The shaman seeks the answer to a specific question, revealed in what is encountered in the trance and, in contrast to ancient tribal ways, questions may now be of a personal nature. Many people join shamanic lodges simply for the purpose of enlightenment and spiritual exploration, although there seem to be increasing numbers of more traditional shamans, involved in soul healing and collective concerns.

PAGANISM

Possibly the fastest-growing religion at the moment is paganism, most simply described as 'nature worship'. 'Pagan' is derived from the Latin *paganus* meaning 'rustic'. There are problems in describing the pagan way because it is by definition non-dogmatic. Paganism embraces many different strands of thought and practice. Perhaps its principal difference from the monotheistic religions is that it is chiefly about what one perceives (on a physical or spiritual level) and what one does, as opposed to what one believes, for belief involves an act of faith. Pagans do not need faith because they sense divinity around them. There are no cult figures, no charismatic leaders and no code of ethics apart from 'Harm none'. Each pagan is her or his own prophet. Far from being a recipe for chaos, pagans believe this promotes tolerance and they point to the many conflicts generated by dogmatic belief systems. Pagans honour divinity in all that is – stones, stars, trees, animals and the earth itself. Seeking to reanimate what is relevant in the wisdom and practices of our forebears, pagans try to get back to our spiritual roots, when a sense of oneness with creation and an inherent sense of meaning and belonging was everyone's inheritance, and to refurbish this in a modern context. Paganism is about joy, celebration and realism in the face of change, death and transformation. It involves a large degree of personal responsibility, for it is not 'cosy' to have no laws cast in marble to indicate what is right or wrong at every juncture.

Pagans love and honour the earth as Mother Goddess, finding joy in the body, as a gift of the Goddess and a powerful sense of the Divine in places of natural beauty. Most pagans use the seasonal cycle as a basis for worship and celebration, and the mythic saga of the mating of the Goddess of the earth with the God as personified by the sun usually forms a background. There are many different paths such as druidry, Wicca/witchcraft (N.B. witchcraft is 'wise-craft' and has nothing to do with satanism or black magic), Northern Tradition and shamanism. Green spirituality is a form of paganism, where ecological awareness, the adoption of sustainable lifestyles and a general concern for the earth and all living species are fostered in a spirit of respect and worship. Of course, a growing interest in recycling, conservation and environment 'friendliness' is present today, quite apart from anything explicitly pagan. However, there are many people who are pretty much pagan, without defining themselves in this way.

In the pagan belief, spirit and matter are not seen as split, but as part of a continuum, so that our bodies and their

pleasures and needs are part of the Divine. One of the most important of pagan ideas is that of the immanence or in-dwelling spirit of the Goddess, within the world and material form, as opposed to an external, autocratic and judgmental deity. Creation and destruction are both contained within the Goddess and Her consort, the God, for both are necessary in a balanced cosmos. The pagan God is mirthful and protective. He discriminates, but lovingly, and He is the hunter at one with His prey, rather than predator or tyrant. Pagan theology is not dualistic, for there is no belief in the devil, or similar. Of course, this does not mean that what we may call 'evil' does not exist, but this can be seen chiefly as a product of alienation from our source. However, paganism is not evangelical, for pagans seek what is right for themselves, rather than what is 'Right' in some eternal, crystallised fashion. Pagans may draw upon many different mythologies – Celtic, Native American, Egyptian, Norse – because, again, it is not a question of one 'right' story but of inspiration and inner quest. Because of the pagan emphasis upon experience, inspiration, respect for the earth and feeling, it can be seen as allied to the Feminine and instinctual, rather than the Masculine, patriarchal and logos-orientated approach of the monotheistic religions.

NEW FEMININE, NEW MASCULINE

Perhaps one of the most important forces at work as the century turns is the revival of the Feminine in many areas. Paganism, with its emphasis upon the personal, the instinctual, the body and the earth is organically a part of this. Many of the ills of the last 2,000 years, and indeed longer, may be laid at the door of the denigration of the Great Feminine, in all Her meanings, both within us and without us. The de-souling of matter as empty, 'unspiritual' and there for the domination and exploitation of Man has led, to a great extent, to our current global plight, our ecological problems and pollution of sea and air. The word 'matter' arises from the same root as 'mother' and 'The World, the Flesh and the Devil' have been grouped together as corrupting and vile. Yet fleshy, worldly things are obsessively attractive as if, denied their ingredient of the sacred, they have indeed become demons, intent on unbalancing us as we strive to subdue, control and possess without ever truly enjoying or respecting. Women, with their greater bodily connection in menstruation, childbirth and sexual seductiveness, their instinctual gifts and their lesser reliance on logos-based thought patterns have been regarded as inferior and often suspect, and such ideas are rooted deeply within our language and conceptual structures. They do not easily yield to legislation and 'political correctness'.

The split between matter and spirit have translated to a rift between science and religion. Until Galileo, science had been more or less under the dominion of the principal religion in Europe, Catholicism. Galileo, although perhaps more of an egotist than a hero, flagged up the existence of scientific 'truth' as distinct from spiritual values, with his *E pur si muove* meaning 'and yet it moves', that is the earth around the sun (which legend tells he uttered at his trial). The ensuing division between scientific investigation and spiritual context has, in a sense, not been beneficial, resulting to some extent in the threats of destruction so well known to us. Rendering 'unto Caesar the things that are Caesar's and unto God the things that are God's seems to have given rise to a moral and conceptual schizophrenia, which is only now giving way to a more holistic perception.

However, I think it is fair to say that dogmatic religious systems owe little to the mystical, creative side of us and that both Galileo and his opponents, the Papacy and the Inquisition, were to a great extent logos and left-brain orientated, which may have contributed to the comparatively lenient treatment Galileo received. It is the right-brain realm, of instinct, pattern perception that has been pushed out of the scene and, in fact, persecuted. We have seen that our brains are bicameral, having a right and left hemisphere, and that the right brain controls creativity, imagination and related faculties, while the left brain is discriminating and logical. This is a concept that we encountered in Chapter 1. The right side of the body is controlled by the left side of the brain and vice versa. In left-handed people it is the right side of the brain that houses the logical facilities. Access to the instinctual side is often found through use of the non-dominant side (i.e. the left hand, in right-handed individuals). Women generally possess greater integration between the brain hemispheres than men and 'women's intuition' is an accepted phenomenon. However, language is a left-brain product, except when used poetically, and it can be an immense struggle to give value and importance to all that may be called 'feminine' by the use of words. One inevitably seems faced with left-brain questions such as 'Yes, but what use is it? Is it right? Is it true?' To the right brain such questions are barely relevant, for definitions are less marked and perceptions more holistic, to return to the word perhaps most relevant of all to the evolving consciousness of the age.

True feminism is about something very different from the militant feminism of previous decades, which can be seen as an aspect of patriarchy. Increasing the numbers of women at board level or in government may do little, if anything at all, to promote the Feminine in its true meaning. The 'New Man' staying at home with the children while his wife brings home the bread may be no better, although economic and social factors that deprive men of their jobs and their status accelerate the process of self-examination and change. 'Patriarchy' signifies 'rule by the fathers' with all this implies, and it persists in some institutions, such as inheritance of title by the first-born son, and allied customs. Women demanding the right to be men hardly enshrines the Feminine. Fortunately, a deeper perception of the Feminine, as relevant both for women and men, is emerging. This is described by Jungian analyst, Marion Woodman, interviewed in Issue 38 of *Caduceus* magazine.

> *Leaving duality means living in paradox. Paradox is the core of wisdom and the core of the Goddess. Wisdom holds the balance of life/death, mind/body, masculine/feminine. Paradox, presence and process are words we associate with the Goddess, she who 'renews everything while herself perduring'.*

Part of the 'new feminine' means acknowledging the intelligence and the spirit within matter and flesh. Honouring the Goddess also means honouring our bodies and the feelings and values that they hold and to which they give mute testimony. By becoming conscious of our 'body wisdom' we can come to know ourselves and to be complete as individuals. By the same token we can become a species living at one with, instead of at war with, Nature, internally and externally. The Feminine honours community rather than hierarchy, unites rather than differentiates, accepts rather than competes. It is not essentially 'better' than masculine approaches, but it is desperately needed to restore balance. All that may be termed 'masculine' has become dry and twisted for lack of it.

The death of Diana, Princess of Wales, at the end of August 1997, had an immense impact and must be considered in the light of the emergence of the Feminine. Several of my friends and acquaintances had dreams of the Morrigan – Irish goddess of war and destruction – or similar figures in the weeks leading up to the horrific crash. Diana's demise had a huge, heartbreaking effect, even upon people totally disinterested in royalty, who tended to take Diana herself 'with a pinch of salt'. However, Diana represented

something powerful and, while this 'something' was diluted in the face of her fallible humanity, when she died its archetypal significance was released in a wave of mourning. The condition of the Feminine was incarnated by Diana, beautiful, graceful, nurturing and maternal. The lack of stability which she sometimes displayed also reflected the destabilisation of the Feminine, as well as its 'legitimate' irrationality. Using undoubted feminine wiles, she stood up alone to the House of Windsor and many forsaken wives, single parents and women with various psychological and emotional disorders thrust upon them by pressures that could be called patriarchal, identified at a human level with the lonely princess. At her death all of these reactions were raised to a higher octave and Diana took on the dimensions of a goddess.

At her funeral her brother pointed out the irony that she was named after the ancient goddess of hunting, but she was herself hounded by the press. However, Roman Diana, also as her Greek counterpart Artemis, was originally much more than merely goddess of the chase. Her province, especially as Artemis, was that of the wild, untamed realms and the creatures that inhabit them, and of a virgin state that implies self-determination in a woman, owned by no man, although she may be sexually active if she so chooses. Like many goddesses, Diana evolved from the ancient model of the Creatrix, powerfully feminine. Diana, Princess of Wales, interestingly was born under the sign of Cancer which is a Water sign, associated with feeling, family and motherhood. Ruled by the moon, usually taken as celestial representative of the Feminine, Cancer has links with the sea and all human emotions for which the sea may be a metaphor. She died at an eclipse, traditionally dangerous for sovereigns – and she was self-designated 'Queen of Hearts'. Marion Woodman suggests that we can bring to consciousness what Diana represented for us by asking ourselves who she was in us, at a profound, archetypal level: 'Why did I weep the tears I wept? Why did I feel that immense wave coming in my belly and feel her go through me? What is it in me that resonates with her vulnerability and her strength?' Diana's death has been seen by some as a metaphor for our times, for all losses, and a 'bad omen' for the millennium. However, I see this as an opportunity for a new outlook and for some important realisations, for her 'sacrifice' can be one of the catalysts that brings fresh and important aspects and powers to light.

In coming to know our bodies and our intuitions at a profound level we more fully understand ourselves and increase our sense of rooted 'self-hood'. Thus, we no longer are so liable to 'fall in love' with denied aspects of ourselves that we see embodied in representatives of the opposite sex, which is what many attractions are about. This makes for greater awareness and maturity in relationships and more space for mature and productive love and growth as opposed to romanticism. By the same token, in making true connection with the physical and the material world, we no longer see the material world as 'out there', a reflection of our own egos, and so we no longer feel impelled to exploit the physical and to seek our status in flashy cars and similar examples of unsustainable living. In response to a growing rootedness that women may feel in their beings, men also can respond by maturing. Men may be conscious of great grief in 'not being needed' in the same way by the women in their life which they may experience and express as anger. However, the Masculine is as necessary as ever, but in a modified and more conscious form. The Feminine, in both women and men (but this may be more accessible to women) states 'This is who I am, this is how I feel, what I value'. However, in order to put this into action, to discriminate, to define what is essential and non-essential, the masculine approach is necessary. As Marion Woodman describes it, 'In . . . discrimination we have the sword . . . The nature Masculine will use it with love. The way of love is the way of the spiritual warrior . . . He has to value, love and protect the inner Feminine'.

Thus, an important and extremely far-reaching vision for the millennium is a new definition and respect for the Feminine that reaches deeper than the cerebral and changes us at a profound level, having implications for our own growth and our relationship with our environment. Along with this arises a new concept of Masculinity that has not lost its incisive quality, but is positive, protective and creative. Although in the late 1990s many inequalities were still afflicting individual women, a true respect for the Feminine is slowly emerging and will probably do more to transform the position of women in the new century than a whole barrage of legislation. The re-emergence of the Feminine is part of our search for balance and the growth that can take us forward into a new phase, and to hold the Masculine and the Feminine, in all their meanings, in balance in awareness may have more than a little relevance in the emergence of a new consciousness in humankind.

GETTING THE MOST FROM THE 'NEW AGE'

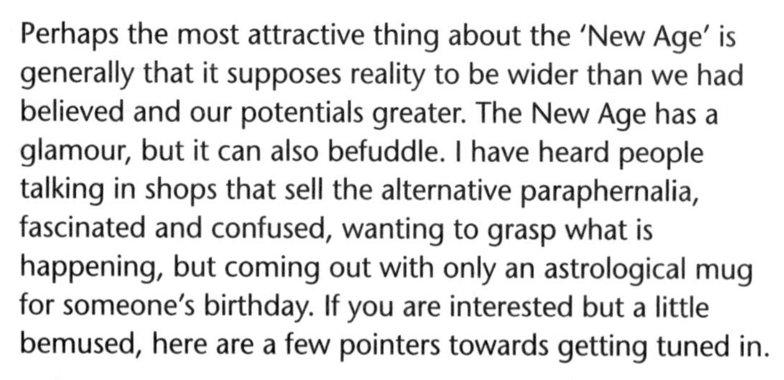

Perhaps the most attractive thing about the 'New Age' is generally that it supposes reality to be wider than we had believed and our potentials greater. The New Age has a glamour, but it can also befuddle. I have heard people talking in shops that sell the alternative paraphernalia, fascinated and confused, wanting to grasp what is happening, but coming out with only an astrological mug for someone's birthday. If you are interested but a little bemused, here are a few pointers towards getting tuned in.

Ornamentation, from butterflies to pentagrams, has extensive symbology that is consciously adopted by many people. However, this doesn't matter at all and you don't have to know what something 'means' in order to decide you like it. Indeed, you will be following your intuition, which is really what the New Age is all about. You can join groups and classes in a spirit of exploration, not total belief. A gentle scepticism is not usually frowned upon, for 'New Agers' usually pride themselves on their tolerance. However, care must naturally be taken to respect the viewpoints and beliefs of others. It is best to start with one subject that interests you and to acquire some information on that, rather than try to take in too many subjects at once. Much of the 'New' Age is, in fact, extremely ancient and simply re-emerging in a new context. Much is diluted and popularised and any search for true enlightenment is long, hard and dedicated work. However, in the shorter term, we can all begin by widening our minds just a little. What you look for in your own corner of the scene should help to enhance your life, make you feel calmer and more harmonious, expand your consciousness, even if only a little at first, and help you to feel something I call 'connectedness' as part of the cosmic web.

You may have an interest in the divinatory arts and may discover an aptitude in yourself – indeed, if you are drawn towards a subject there is a fair chance that this may be the case. If you feel a general wish to learn more, the remarks below may help you decide which avenue to pursue. If you wish to consult a practitioner of one of the divinatory arts, it is as well to think and choose carefully. You may want to know your 'fortune' but a more positive motive may be to understand yourself and what is happening better, so you can attune to changes, avert some troubles and take a creative approach. Make sure that this is on offer. A reputable person will seek to help and guide rather than make a stunning prediction but, none the less, if you ask to know something you need to be sure you can handle the answer. Do you want to hear that your current relationship is unlikely to last, that changes and challenges are on the way, that money will be a struggle? This is what you may hear, although you should also get encouragement and support. Most practitioners consider it unhelpful and unethical to predict death and ruin, but some do and, while they may well be wrong, can you cope with such a fright? Not all practitioners are as talented as they make out and many psychic fairs are permeated by an atmosphere of greed and trickery. It is relatively easy to pick up clairvoyantly on someone's hopes and fears, for they 'hang in the air' around them. (It is also possible to form accurate judgements by noticing small details like rings, clothing and mannerisms.) Prediction of the future is a rarer skill.

THE MANTIC ARTS

The principal mantic arts are astrology, tarot, I Ching, runes, numerology and palmistry, although there are many other forms of divination. I would say that clairvoyance (i.e. 'clear sight' which perceives the hidden) is operative in those who practise these, at least to some degree. However, some astrologers and numerologists might object to this view. Clairvoyance can operate with far fewer trappings, for instance simply through gazing into a crystal until the 'Younger Self' or the perceptive, 'primitive' part of the mind begins to form pictures. The more complex mantic arts may simply serve as a distraction to the logical mind, while the intuition does its stuff. Opinions on this vary, however.

Astrology

Astrology is based on the 'As above, so below' principle. Movements of the sun, moon and planets correlate with events on earth and to personality traits. Astrologers do not usually see the planetary movements as causing us to do or be certain things. Many astrologers think more synchronistically; there is something that links us with the cosmos, but it is outside the realm of cause and effect. This is in line with the views of C.G. Jung, founder of analytical psychology, who studied astrology. Some statistical studies have supported the beliefs of astrology, for example the work of Jeff Mayo, which proved that there is a correlation between introversion and the Water signs (Cancer, Scorpio, Pisces) and Earth signs (Taurus, Virgo and Capricorn) contrasting with the Air signs (Gemini, Libra and Aquarius) and Fire signs (Aries, Leo and Sagittarius) which are biased towards extroversion. The studies of the French statistician, Michel Gauquelin, showed that certain planetary positions tended towards prominence in certain professions (e.g. Mars on the horizon at birth for the military). Some observations suggest that causation, at least in part, may be at work, for instance Maurice Cotterell's work with sunspots and the solar wind, mentioned in Chapter 5. The jury is still out regarding why astrology is effective. Most astrologers feel this is irrelevant. They say astrology is based upon observation and it works.

Popular astrology is based on sun signs, that is the zodiacal sign occupied by the sun at the time you were born. Almost everyone, regardless of their expressed opinion of astrology, knows their sun sign and even its major characteristics. Because of a phenomenon known as 'precession' where the earth wobbles on its axis, the signs no longer coincide with the constellations, but this has little significance, for astrology is/was based upon observation, and it is just as likely that the constellations were named after observed effects, than conjured up from star formations. The sun sign forms a background colouring and most people are noticeably like their sun sign, although, of course, we are all individuals and variations in personality are almost infinite and are depicted in the full birth chart. Predictions on the basis of sun sign are much more questionable, although they prevail in the popular press. The more specific they may be the more obviously they are suspect – for instance one-twelfth of the population cannot really expect to win a substantial sum of money during the same day/week or to start a passionate new romance.

Proper astrology is based on the entire birth chart, a 'sky-map' of the planets, sun and moon and several other factors, drawn up not only for the day you were born but for the time and place also, although a reasonable amount of information can be gleaned even when the time of birth is unknown. From this, an astrologer can ascertain the basic dynamics of your personality and make a prediction for the coming year, based upon the correlation of current planetary movements with those present at birth, and using other techniques. Predictions are rarely specific, more usually about trends and emphasis placed upon helping the client to become more self-aware and to adjust. Astrology can also be used to elect a propitious time to begin an enterprise (electional astrology) or to obtain the answer to a question, find a lost object or similar (horary astrology). Some astrologers are 'psychological', others have a more traditional approach, but medieval fatalism is not encountered with good astrologers. Many astrologers will have spent a long time training and studying and may have qualifications from the Faculty of Astrological Studies, Company of Astrologers or similar body, although this is a profession for mavericks and many good astrologers have no qualification. Go by recommendation, expect to spend upwards of an hour with your astrologer, possibly considerably longer, and be prepared for professional charges, for studying a birth chart can take a long time. Be sure that your astrologer knows what you want from the consultation (e.g. greater awareness in relationships, career advice, what the future holds) and intends to provide it. Astrological chart interpretations can be obtained by computer and are much less personal and skilled, although they may be useful. You may consider studying astrology yourself if you are interested in planetary symbols, are good at translating symbolic meanings into everyday and if you have a strong feeling that we have a connection with the cosmos.

Tarot

Tarot cards are believed to have first appeared in Europe, in Northern Italy, during the fourteenth century. Prior to this their origins are believed to be Eastern, or Egyptian. The tarot pack consists of 22 Major Arcana cards and 56 Minor Arcana, divided into four suits: wands, swords, pentacles and cups. Wands are sometimes called rods or batons, pentacles coins and cups chalices, and there are other variations that proliferate as tarot becomes more popular. Each of the Major Arcana displays a powerfully allegorical or archetypal image, such as The High Priestess, The Tower, The Fool or The Hermit, which evokes a train of associations in the mind of the diviner. The symbolism of the Minor Arcana may be less dramatic. Each of the suits relates to areas of life or experience, wands pertaining to career or enterprise, pentacles to money and material resources, cups to emotional life and swords to the area of the mentality and often to disputes. Each of the suits is numbered 1 to 10, with four 'court cards' King, Queen, Knight and Page, which often represent actual people, or may be selected to represent the querent (i.e. person who is there for the consultation) in a spread. After a question has been formulated, the cards are shuffled and picked, and they set out in a chosen pattern, or 'spread', with certain placements indicating certain times or areas in the life of the querent. There are many varieties of spreads, such as the Celtic Cross, Astrological Spread or simple yes/no arrangement. However, many people use the cards more informally, picking three or four and interpreting those as seems fit.

Tarot imagery is vivid and stunning. There are many and growing varieties of tarot pack to suit the orientation of the practitioner, such as pagan, Celtic, astrological, Egyptian, and even a Tarot of the Cat People. Beginners are sometimes advised to choose the basic pack, the Rider-Waite, to get to know the symbols, moving on to something more personal as experience is gained. Tarot is most often used for fortune telling, but it is much more than that. Each of the Major Arcana cards can, and should, be explored by a process of meditation and visualisation, so that the practitioner can arrive at a personal understanding of the meaning of the symbols. Each of the Major Arcana cards corresponds to a path on the Qabalistic Tree of Life. The Qabala is an ancient Hebrew mystical doctrine and the Tree of Life is a diagram of manifestation, representing the emergence into form of anything, from an idea to the cosmos itself. It consists of ten sephiroth or spheres, each representing a stage or characteristic in the emergence of Form from Idea, or Divinity, or from the material world upwards towards the sphere of pure energy, that is evolution returning to Source. Twenty-two paths interconnect the sephiroth. These paths can be explored in 'Pathworking' which is a system of guided visualisation. Thus, the tarot is part of an ancient wisdom teaching.

Tarot readers obviously vary, from 'Madame Zara' in the fairground to those who offer counselling, insight and a context of spiritual progression. A good tarot reader is less preoccupied with telling you 'what will happen' than in pointing out alternatives and opportunities for growth. If you wish for a tarot reading, follow personal recommendation if possible, or choose someone with whom you feel good and who affects few glamorous trappings. Tarot symbolism comes more complete than astrological symbolism, which has to be built up from a variety of complex factors, thus tarot may be seen as less cerebral. Because of this it appeals to some people more than to others. Tarot is certainly a beautiful system. You may like to study tarot if you are readily able to relate complex symbols to everyday life, can marry up pictures with circumstances, find that pictures activate 'hunches' and are prepared to develop your intuition.

I Ching

This is an ancient Chinese divination system, more cryptic and subtle than tarot, based on the principles of yin and yang. The I Ching is also known as The Book of Change, for change is the only constant in the universe. Composed before 1000 BCE it arises from the heart of ancient Chinese wisdom and enshrines the notion that the person who understands the laws of transformation can attain freedom through identification with destiny. Generated from an entire philosophic tradition, the I Ching is immensely complex. Today, we use it for divination, as we understand the term, although there is that within the ancient Chinese approach which invites us to deepen and to examine meanings, becoming more distant from our day-to-day desires.

The I Ching consists of 64 hexagrams, made up from differing combinations of six broken and unbroken lines. Broken lines signify yin (i.e. receptive, feminine energy), unbroken lines signify yang (i.e. outgoing, masculine energy). The oracle can be composed by throwing coins or picking yarrow stalks, to signify broken or unbroken lines. The resulting hexagram can then be looked up in the I Ching oracle. As an example, the tenth hexagram is composed of five yang lines and one yin. It is called 'Lu' or Treading Carefully. One interpretation is 'Lu suggests the idea of one treading on the tail of a tiger which doesn't bite him. There will be progress and success. Hazardous position – no distress or failure'.

It can be seen from this that the I Ching is not an easy system to use if one wants straight answers that apply to modern life. It requires considerable reflection and to some extent invites a shift in consciousness, both in practitioner

and consultee, although, as with all systems, these may be one and the same person! The I Ching can sometimes be staggeringly to the point and at others extremely obscure. You may prefer to consult an I Ching practitioner if you wish to achieve something of a philosophic understanding as well as prediction. You may like to study it if you are attracted to Chinese thought and wish to develop intuition in the context of wisdom and wider understanding.

Numerology

The study of numerology presupposes that numbers possess meaning over and above mere quantity, and that they also have a qualitative tone. Knowledge and insight can be gained through the interpretation of numbers derived from date of birth or name. The former may be arrived at by adding together the digits of the birthday until they have been reduced to a single-digit number (i.e. 9 or below) and then interpreting that number. As an example, 28 March 1979 is written as 28.3.1979 = 2+8+3+1+9+7+9=39, 3+9=12, 1+2=3. The birth number in this case is 3 and this is believed to convey certain information about character and destiny on the basis of 'threeness': 3 is, in fact, a creative, playful number, relating to father–mother–child. Extensive interpretation can stem from this. In the case of names, each letter is converted to a number, A=1, B=2, and so on, up to I=9 and the returning to J=1. This can be complex, for different names signify different areas of the personality. For instance, a pet name will indicate how the person operates in an intimate situation, while the letters of the signature will indicate a more formal context, vowels may indicate heart, consonants external matters, etc. In ancient systems, such as the Hebrew, where numbers were also letters, the system was perhaps easier, but our modern, mechanical methods seem at a greater distance from the mystical. None the less, numerology has a respectable pedigree arising from (and, no doubt, before) Pythagoras, and number and proportion are central to the construction of the universe in a way not conveyed in school mathematics. Numbers underpin our lives, and our birth date, for instance, is a number that we carry with us all our lives.

The numerologist John Burford, author of *Numerology and Relationships – A Beginner's Guide* (Hodder & Stoughton, 1998) has told me that babies born in the new millennium will bring with them a simpler, purer vibration. For instance, the birthdate 1.1.2000 reduces to 1+1+2+0+0+0, which adds quite simply to 4. A similar pattern arises with many birthdays (e.g. 3.4.2000 reduces immediately to 9). Further into the new century, this will still be happening, with such birth dates as 3.2.2001 which adds up to 8, and so forth. As these children grow and take their place in society we may see the effects of a less complex or clearer vision, brought by them and taking its effect on jaded, old systems.

Numerology will appeal to you if you feel there is a beauty and a pattern to number, and that numbers contain mystical secrets. Much can be gleaned simply, as outlined here, but the entire subject is much more complex, if one wishes to go that far. Numerology consultants are not common. Predictions may be made on the basis of the current year number resonating with your own, and on other factors. As with all consultants, recommendation is your best recourse, to avoid being misled, alarmed or wasting your time.

Palmistry

As the name implies, palmistry deduces character and future events from markings on the palm, length of fingers, size of mounds, etc. It operates according to set principles, for example if your Mount of Venus, on your palm, at the base of the thumb, is high, rounded and firm, then your vitality and sex drive are high; if your third or Apollo finger is long and straight then you are artistic and successful.

Predictions are encoded in lines, for instance horizontal lines at the base of the little finger denote relationships, vertical lines denote children, etc.

As with all the mantic arts, interpretations can be sensibly modified. A short life-line might be fatalistically interpreted to mean a short life, but that has been shown not to be the case, for short life-lines appear on the hands of octogenarians. So this short line may mean a restricted life, a life of lowered vitality or perhaps a simple life. In addition, the Line of Life (which runs around the Mount of Venus) can be strengthened by a line running inside and parallel, indicating increased vitality and resistance. There are ways to measure the passage of time on the palm, so markings on the lines of Life or Fate (which runs towards the large finger), such as breaks, stars and circles, can be linked to an event due to happen at a certain point in the life. Many people object to this, finding it hard to accept that events in the life almost from birth could be mapped out on the palm. However, markings on the palm do change over time, and so a mark may disappear or appear according to the modification of the lifestyle, perhaps. Lines on or proportions of the palm and fingers can be an expression of body wisdom, as if we know in our skin and bones what will be and what we truly are, although our minds may ignore it. There is some scientific corroboration for some aspects of palmistry; for instance, the Mount of Venus has been asserted to have physical nerve connections with the arteries going into the heart. Some palmistry tenets are common sense, for instance a firm, pink palm indicates good health and strength, whereas a pale, sweaty one indicates low vitality, nerves, etc.

Like everything else, palmistry depends to a great extent upon intuition. If a personal approach appeals to you, or you like to be able to tell a lot about a person from appearance, then palmistry may be your subject. As a quick method, yielding lots of subliminal information to the person who holds your palm, it can be degraded to the 'fairground' type of approach, although there are some highly skilled and helpful palm readers. Personal recommendation is best.

Runes

Runes are most easily defined as the old alphabet of the Vikings. However, like all ancient forms of writing, they mean more than just letters. The mere act of conveying information via the written word involves a change in consciousness from the days when word of mouth predominated and is, in a sense, magical, being transformative. Runes are also magical symbols in that they convey much more than a sound made by the mouth or part of a word. Each rune is part of a set of correspondences, including colours, animals, planets, life events and many more. In answer to a question runes can be 'cast' usually on a cloth kept especially for that purpose. A chosen number of runes is withdrawn from the bag in which they are kept and cast down. The way they fall may be interpreted, or they may be placed on a chart.

Runes are simple symbols that mean a great deal. Each rune can be said to mean as much as a card in the Major Arcana of the tarot, but you have to conjure up that meaning yourself. For instance, the rune Berkana is a shape like an angular B. However, it brings with it myriad associations, such as the birch tree, the sign of Cancer, the colour green, fertility, the home, to name but a few. Runes may appeal to you if you are of a tactile nature, liking to touch the stone or wood upon which the runes are engraved. They will also suit you if you prefer to arrive at your own images, from a simple symbol, and if you are able to remember and make meaningful links with all the appropriate associations with each rune. Runes can also be used as an alternative to ordinary writing, for the making of charms and amulets. If you are serious about using runes, each rune should be meditated upon, so the meaning comes through personally, to you. In choosing someone to cast the runes for you, the same criteria should be used as with other practitioners; common sense, kindness, helpfulness and personal recommendation.

Graphology

This is the art of reading character in the handwriting. As far as I am aware, there are no techniques for predicting the future through this. Handwriting can be analysed to discover personality traits from many factors, from the slope of the writing (backward slope may indicate a more introverted or self-orientated personality while forward-tilted writing indicates an outgoing nature, broadly speaking) through the setting out of the page down to literal dotting of i's and crossing of t's. It is not hard to accept that our style of writing could indicate our personality – for instance, if we are under stress we tend to push harder with the pen, and if we are in a hurry our letters tend to be partly formed. Now that writing in a certain manner is not insisted upon by schoolteachers, there has emerged the opportunity to express ourselves in the way we write – and to give away secrets about ourselves! Like astrology, graphology is being taken seriously by some employers who are subjecting the applications of prospective employees to analysis, prior to making a decision. If you are interested to find out more about friends and family without probing for information, all you need is a sample of handwriting and knowledge of graphology to obtain much information. Graphology may appeal if you have a fairly analytical and painstaking approach, for there are lots of factors to be weighed in the balance.

In a modern context all the mantic arts are truly about understanding and growth rather than out-and-out prediction. Our modern mind-set is not fatalistic, as in medieval days, but concentrates on improvement and expansion. This may be, in part, because we do not want to face bad things. However, it is possible that, due to our increasing openness and wish to expand our consciousness, we are really less 'fated' than we were. The purpose of prophecy must surely be to avert disaster, rather than to be correct. Of course, we are largely slaves to our circumstances and make-up, and any real freedom is hard won. None the less, it is possible. Viewing ourselves in a cosmic context is part of the philosophy behind the mantic arts, and this will surely become more prevalent in the twenty-first century. Along with this, our acquisition of real freedom is likely to increase.

EXPLORING THE MYSTERIOUS

Many people are now especially intent on exploring the unexplained or on finding new meanings in our environment. Whatever your interests, there are not only plenty of publications to be found on every subject, but there are also many clubs and societies formed to help members exchange ideas and experiences. If you are interested in UFOs, for example, you should have little difficulty tracking down those people of a like mind. However, if your interests are more diffuse, and you have had little opportunity to explore conceptually, you may not be fully aware of what is available.

Earth mysteries

Of fascination to many people, the general topic of earth mysteries has drawn attention. This is most generally based on the belief that there are hidden 'energies' within the earth, with all this implies about the activities of our forebears and our contemporary experience. However, some earth mysteries' aficionados are scornful of this notion, favouring an archaeological, anthropological and historical approach. Earth mysteries unites all such

approaches to our earth, from the sacred to the scientific. Dowsing is an activity favoured by many people interested in the esoteric aspect of earth mysteries, for it is possible to dowse for energy patterns within the earth, and this is a skill that most people possess, to some degree. If you have a sense of something special in certain locations, are fascinated by what lies behind the construction of Stonehenge, the Pyramids and such like, feel there are mysteries encoded in the landscape or that the earth is alive, then there may well be something for you in this study.

Feng shui

Extending in a sense from earth mysteries is the Chinese art of feng shui. Literally meaning 'wind, water', feng shui is about the arrangement of the environment to maximise our good fortune and enhance all aspects of our lives. It arises from the concept of space being an expression of energy and that we resonate with and are affected by our surroundings. In truth, it is part of a complex philosophical Chinese system, connected with the I Ching. Having said this, feng shui is a practical and adaptable system, most applicable to modern, Western life, and it is extremely popular, taken seriously by people who have little or no interest in the mystical. Artistic and common-sensical as well as esoteric, the principles of feng shui can make a great deal of difference to the success and fulfilment of our lives and businesses if we incorporate them into our homes and places of work. If you are conscious of a strong resonance with your environment and feel life could be improved by more harmonious surroundings; if you feel there are secrets to arranging decor that go beyond lifestyle catalogues, then feng shui is likely to interest you.

Crystals

One way of altering our environment in a subtle fashion may be to include crystals. Many belief systems assert that crystals are alive. They are popular in the 'New Age' and can be used to alter the subtle climate of a room. For instance, crystals absorb electromagnetic vibrations and so may be useful placed above the television. Crystals can be used for healing, or to store energy. In addition to being pretty, crystals can be powerful things and their influence is not always beneficial, especially in the bedroom. The subject of crystals is vast, and may appeal especially to persons of a tactile nature. If you are especially attracted to crystals and feel there is 'something about them' there is plenty of opportunity to discover more.

Colour

Colour has a profound effect upon the way we feel and can be consciously used to alter moods, to create an atmosphere or to heal us. There is a body of information and knowledge concerning the subtle and far-reaching effects that colour can have upon us.

Earth mysteries, feng shui, crystals, colour – these are just some of the subjects that reflect our greater awareness of the world around us, both in its power to affect us at a variety of levels and for a certain mysterious quality or sentience, that is altering our perception of life.

COUNSELLING

Truly a phenomenon of the late twentieth century, there are plenty of clichés associated with counselling. The television series *Star Trek, the Next Generation* has a counsellor, Deanna Troi, as part of the crew of the *Enterprise*, and it has been said that this fact alone will serve to date the series more than any other. Deanna is an Empath, her mother coming from the planet Beta Zed, where telepathy is standard. However, Counsellor Troi senses emotions in the

way many present-day, terrestrial counsellors are trained to do, although picking up on the feelings of strange life-forms is still beyond the skill of most!

The purpose of counselling is not to take away emotional pain, for that is often not possible, certainly in the short term. However, pain may be made easier to bear, through understanding and support. The sheer benefit of 'just talking about it' is not to be underestimated. In contrast to even the dearest friend, a counsellor will never claim attention for her or his own problems but is there solely for the client, concentrating totally on what is being expressed and reflecting it back, where appropriate, to foster greater understanding. Psychotherapy is similar to counselling and it is hard to define where one begins and the other finishes. However, in general, psychotherapy lasts longer, works more deeply and usually more often, with several sessions per week taking the place of the usual weekly counselling session.

Counsellors work in a variety of different ways and levels. A psychodynamic counsellor works on the basis of the belief that there is a subconscious mind and that movement is possible between the subconscious and the conscious, thus material may be used in order to reveal subconscious workings, including the dynamics between counsellor and client. This can be uncomfortable, but also instructive. Humanistic counsellors seek to discover each person's potential and help them to build upon it, strengthening talent and individuality. Behaviourists will work on a certain behaviour that needs to be corrected, such as a phobia, without concentrating on the underlying cause. This can be effective in the short term, but some people believe that the problem will merely resurface in another form. Cognitive work focuses upon ideas and concepts, which can provide a helpful framework, but change at an emotional level may take longer. There are many types of counselling approach, including some that incorporate massage, hypnotherapy and other treatments. Some counsellors specialise in couple work, in which case the purpose is to clarify issues and create a safe space for discussion, not to provide a magic solution to difficulties.

If you decide you would like to see a counsellor, you are quite within your rights to ask that person how he or she works and whether your particular problem is likely to respond. Although your experience of counselling will be a little uncomfortable at times, if much is to be accomplished, you are entitled to feel basically at ease with your counsellor. It can be disempowering to be a client, for it naturally evokes childlike feelings of dependency. Your counsellor will be aware of this. However, do not let this position affect your power of choice. Not every counsellor is right for every client. It may be best to shop around, having an exploratory session possibly with several counsellors before deciding on one that makes you feel comfortable. Counselling can and should enhance your self-awareness, your understanding of your life situations and eventually your ability to cope, but sometimes this takes a long time and things can sometimes get worse before they get better, depending upon how deep-seated a problem may be.

In order to get the best out of counselling it may be necessary for you to be prepared to change at a profound level, to examine totally new perspectives on what appeared safe and cosy in your world, and to feel at times that the whole thing is hard work, challenging and hitting you on the raw. However, I would also say that the analytical, extremely detached approach of some therapists is not favourite when you are going through a tough patch and need support. The danger here is that you may become a dependent victim and the therapist may take on the role of judgemental parent. The therapist should address this thoroughly, and help you move through it. None the less, I have seen more than one unfortunate soul waste miserable years and lots of hard cash simply getting worse. That is a worst possible scenario and not common.

However, it is as well to remember that therapists aren't always right just because they're therapists and because some inferiority complex that you have shouts that they have all the answers and you have none. Facing some things deep within can feel quite shredding, but if the therapy is unremittingly gruelling and you feel no sense of warmth and support, give yourself permission to get out.

One of the most important functions of counselling is that it can enable negative emotions to become fully conscious and expressed. In this way, we do not deceive ourselves, nor are we controlled by what we have not acknowledged. As we evolve into the twenty-first century this is vital. Counselling is a two-way commitment and if you are to get the most out of it you will certainly need to work at it. In the end, counselling can give you valuable insight into life and personality, but it is not a panacea. The ideal is 'manageable' rather than 'perfect'. Freud called it 'the talking cure' and certainly, for all the chatter, we rarely talk – or listen – enough. At the new millennium, enhanced appreciation of the value of life and concern for our fellows make the ideas within counselling even more valuable. However, these are old skills revamped for self-exploration and Mother Wit has been facilitated in many ways down through the ages by village wise-woman and temple priest/ess.

SELF-EXPANSION

Increasingly, avenues are offered for us to expand ourselves, not merely in being more effectual, self-aware, positive and so on, but to extend our consciousness. We may wish to increase our extrasensory awareness, to make inner journeys through visualisation, to change consciousness through meditation, to work with our dreams or to practise certain techniques, such as astral projection, channelling or awakening our chakras. Shamanism, or the practice of spirit flight, is another technique increasingly explored and a context of Native American wisdom is often adopted, although shamanic traditions exist in all indigenous cultures and it may be equally valid to explore ancient Celtic pathways of the soul. Native wisdom is increasingly sought and cultivated, for it is becoming apparent that we have lost more than we have gained in our technological society and there are plenty of opportunities to explore these avenues for anyone who wishes to do so.

The astral body is believed to be a subtle body whose essence interpenetrates the ordinary body but which is capable of separating from it, especially in sleep. Astral travelling is the art of consciously projecting ourselves outside our bodies, by inducing a certain state of mind. Dreams are a pathway to the unconscious and may tell us much about ourselves, or may be prophetic. We are well advised to record our dreams and ask ourselves what they may mean. The chakras can be described as 'organs' or energy centres in the subtle body. These can be activated and energised, resulting in enhanced perceptions and vitality. Channelling is the ability to 'channel' messages that are believed to come from the spirit world, or other dimensions. Naturally, to develop any of these skills is an enormous expansion of ourselves, but they are not without risks. If you wish to open the doors of perception and to discover new abilities in yourself, you will be naturally attracted to such fields. One of the greatest pitfalls here is the ego and it is fair to say that if you embark upon any such path just to satisfy your ego, you court disaster. Naturally, none of us is without ego, but experiencing ego-gratification at successful channelling or astral projection is a far cry from doing it *just* for that, and in any case needs to be monitored carefully. It is possible to delude oneself and those without strong egos or sense of self, including those with inflated egos, may run the risk of disintegrating to some extent. This is not to discourage any seekers, but it is a reminder that all such practices are legacies of ancient mystery schools whose criteria and training were extremely rigorous. Here, there is wisdom and enlightenment, but dabbling isn't recommended.

HEALING

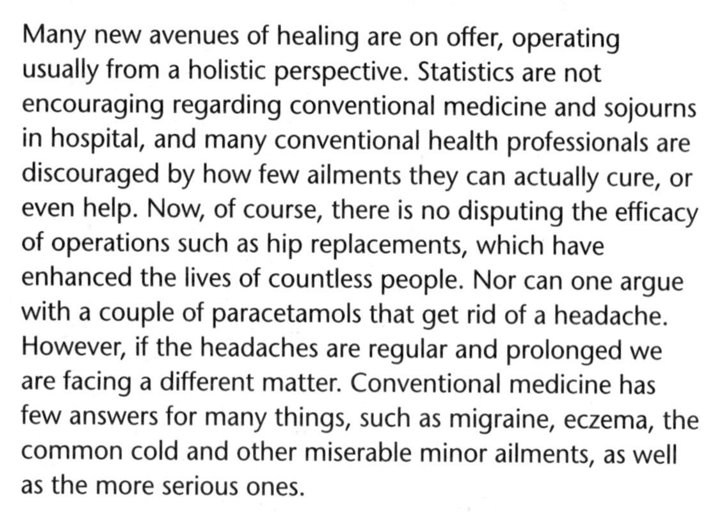

Many new avenues of healing are on offer, operating usually from a holistic perspective. Statistics are not encouraging regarding conventional medicine and sojourns in hospital, and many conventional health professionals are discouraged by how few ailments they can actually cure, or even help. Now, of course, there is no disputing the efficacy of operations such as hip replacements, which have enhanced the lives of countless people. Nor can one argue with a couple of paracetamols that get rid of a headache. However, if the headaches are regular and prolonged we are facing a different matter. Conventional medicine has few answers for many things, such as migraine, eczema, the common cold and other miserable minor ailments, as well as the more serious ones.

Of course, it is common sense to consult your health professional if you are ill. However, those who find that medical science cannot identify or treat the true problem effectively (e.g. migraine), or who feel that the cure is more deadly than the disease (as with some cancer treatments), or who feel that they need something of an overhaul, rather than intervention, or who are aiming for optimum health rather than absence of disease, may wish to turn to alternative therapies. These may include:

- **Acupuncture** – the ancient Chinese system of altering the energy currents in the body by inserting needles at special points.

- **Aromatherapy** – the use of essential oils and massage. The scent of the oil acts in a subtle way upon the body to promote healing and massage is likewise beneficial.
- **Reflexology** – this works on the principle that the soles of the feet are connected to all parts of the body and works on them by massage, to effect change and healing.
- **Osteopathy** – manipulating the skeleton to cure bad back, migraine, etc.
- **Chiropractic** – in some ways similar to osteopathy, but concentrating on the spine.
- **Herbalism** – using herbs to treat ailments, using old knowledge that has been sidelined in many cases.
- **Homoeopathy** – using like to treat like, this is a subtle but effective means of cure, where tiny amounts of a substance that could *cause* the malady are ingested, achieving a cure presumably on the same principle as immunisation, but with less interference with the immune system.
- **Hypnotherapy** – providing access to the subconscious by the induction of trance, so enabling the psychosomatic cause of some conditions to be discovered and/or removed.
- **Spiritual healing** – this operates outside the physical realm, assuming disease originates in the subtle realms. Some healers regard themselves as channellers of healing energy, but there are various ways of visualising this. **Reiki** is a form of spiritual healing. It is supposed that there is more at work here than simple 'faith healing' and some results would certainly seem to bear this out.

There is no space here to detail all forms of alternative medicine and their application. Obviously, this is a vast subject. Some people have derived tremendous benefit from such therapies. In general, it would seem they are safer than conventional medicine, but that does not mean they cannot do harm, for they can and people have been injured by incompetent osteopathy or massage – and certain herbs can kill. Any practitioner should be well-qualified and have good references. In general, it may be said that most ailments will at least improve if subjected to the correct alternative remedy, and sometimes it is the practitioner who has the healing influence, not so much the treatment. Alternative health treatments are helpful, offering hope to many and sometimes producing what amounts to miracles. There is no absolute 'answer to everything'. Exploration, an open mind and a commitment to responsibility and self-help are part of the picture.

EXPLORING FURTHER

This chapter has attempted a run-down of subjects that could fill many bookshelves. Readers who wish to explore further will find all the subjects mentioned, apart from types of healing, covered in one of the volumes in the *Beginner's Guide* series, published by Hodder & Stoughton (see Further Reading for details).

The New Age may contain a few red herrings, but its ethos is inspired by the need to progress conceptually and spiritually. It may be dismissed by some as an ageing hippie phenomenon empowered by 1960s' drop-outs, or simply wishful thinking by a lunatic fringe. However, it is really about a genuine seeking for new approaches *because the old ones blatantly do not work any more.* This isn't empty self-deception that could be put back on track by a return to 'family values' and the Victorian work ethic. To attribute modern ills to a loss of values and to suggest a return to conventional lifestyles or religion is to miss the point. People have stopped following these because they have ceased to have meaning, because their limitations have become obvious and because something more expansive, inspiring and relevant is needed, and to assert otherwise may be to fall into the trap of dogmatism or fundamentalism. Here, we have a genuine response to a failing system. Many of the ideas are bound to be half-baked, naïve or delusory. However, it is written that by walking around in enough confusion is the way to enlightenment found. 'Love and light' is the motto of the age. True, some of the love is self-love and the light may be a mirage, but a sense of community and widening horizons that we approach together is growing, with bonds of affection forged in groups who do at least strive to be as conscious as possible. In the last analysis, bonds of love and community, where we consent to be the keeper of our sisters and brothers are our soundest bastions against millenarian changes. What's new?

7

ATLANTIS, THE PYRAMIDS AND MUCH MORE

'Tis strange, – but true; for truth is always strange;
Stranger than fiction: if it could be told,
How much would novels gain by the exchange!

BYRON, *DON JUAN*

It is only with the heart that one can see rightly; what is essential is invisible to the eye.

ANTOINE DE ST EXUPERY

> *Life is the art of drawing sufficient conclusions from insufficient premises.*
>
> SAMUEL BUTLER

In a sense, much of this chapter is personal because it contains material which relates to a personal search or inner conviction. This 'conviction' is that there is some basic secret, some unifying principle that underlies much that is mysterious and unexplained, from the pyramids to telepathy; that this 'secret' is, in a sense, open and obvious but for some reason we cannot see it and in it lies what could be called our salvation, because it can free us not only from the drawbacks of our belief systems and our uncontrolled emotions which lead us to harm each other, but also from dependence on crude and harmful ways of generating energy, such as fossil fuels. Indeed, far more is possible, amounting to a rebirth of the consciousness of humankind. This has to do with our basic understanding of the energies that underpin life and that lie beneath 'reality' as we know it, and it is also linked to our concepts regarding our own essence, and our evolution. There exists sound evidence that some of our assumptions regarding our history are wrong and there are also extremely speculative viewpoints that are quite at variance with history and even reality, as we know it. While it is foolish to take on trust every wild and wonderful story, I believe it may also be equally foolish to dismiss out of hand anything that threatens to overthrow the cherished scheme of reality. An open mind is an open door to the undiscovered country.

My 'unifying principle' may simply be the union of the right and left hemispheres of the brain, which, as we have seen, house an 'artist' and a 'scientist' respectively. However, in a sense that is an explanation that explains little, for what might actually happen when these are united, when instinct and logic really do work together? How does it feel to have both systems balanced and not only functioning harmoniously but both operating to a highly advanced standard? Could this not result in something that is greater than the sum of its parts? And what might be the practical results of this truly holistic consciousness as it impacted upon the individual and the environment? I have long had a 'feeling' that shape and vibration were important factors in this 'open secret' and I received an exciting hint about this in a lecture given in 1997 by the writer and Egyptologist, David Elkington.

THE POWER OF SOUND

David told us that the civilisation of Egypt is 10,000 years older than we have hitherto believed, and that the Eye of Horus is more than an icon; it is an important ancient measurement, based on the proportions of the skull and having vital relationship to the workings of acoustics. The oscillations of sound are measured in spirals, found carved in such places as the prehistoric temple of Newgrange, in Northern Ireland, where the sun's rays pierce the depths at the winter solstice, and at Wayland's Smithy in Oxfordshire, England, and many other similar ancient monuments, and this could indicate that people we regard as primitive actually possessed highly developed knowledge. I have written elsewhere about the spiral as a significator of the passage of spirit, specifically that of the Goddess, into the manifest world and out once more. The spiral may have a more specific meaning, which does not detract from its poetical and metaphorical connotations which may be a necessary part of the picture. David also told us that the ancient Egyptians had used the power of sound in ways that we cannot imagine and that they had used it to raise the cyclopean blocks that form the pyramids and other structures, such as the Sphinx temples, with engineering skill that we do not possess today. Sound vibrations raised these great stones – I can reveal the amazing fact that this method has now been successfully repeated by David and his colleagues, using the tone A flat which also has a calming influence on the human brain. How this was accomplished, together with much new and highly fascinating material, is to be the subject of David's forthcoming book, *Jesus BC* to be published through Curtis Brown in the spring of 1999. A television series is also planned. However, before we further explore Egypt and its enigmas, let us tread less charted ground.

ATLANTIS

The mere mention of the word 'Atlantis' is enough to destroy the reputation of any serious scholar. The bed of the Atlantic has now been so thoroughly mapped that it seems unlikely that a lost continent could lie there. The discovery of a regular pattern of gigantic stones underwater, near the Bimini Islands, seeming to form part of an ancient ceremonial road, coincided with the predictions of the clairvoyant, Edgar Cayce, who foretold that Atlantis would rise again at the time of the discovery (i.e. 1968–9). However, as we have seen, prophecy can be unreliable and the clairvoyant may merely have been picking up the relatively unimportant fact that the *story* of Atlantis would rise again. Although the blocks of stone have been worked in a way that indicates they are not a product of nature, there exists no conclusive evidence that they are the remains of the controversial vanished civilisation. None the less, I do not feel that the existence of a literal Atlantis has been disproved. If it is true that the earth has been visited by catastrophes such as pole shift and collision with meteors, as many respectable scientists agree, then it hardly seems impossible that a mighty civilisation could vanish almost without trace, many miles below the ocean bed. For instance, oyster shells found in the region of Lake Titicaca, on the border of Bolivia and Peru, indicate that the lake

must once have been at sea level and that some cataclysm in the remost past raised it to its present level 4 km (2.5 miles) higher.

There is, however, no reason why this lost continent should ever have been situated in what is now the Atlantic, for it is quite possible that it lay elsewhere, specifically at the South Pole in the days when it was temperate and not buried under a thick sheet of ice. This is strongly suggested by old maps called 'portolans' such as the map of the Turkish pirate, beheaded in 1554, called the Piri Re'is map, which shows the contours of Antarctica. In fact, there exist many such maps, disregarded by scholars as peppered with medieval inaccuracy, and study of their composition indicates that the standard of accuracy actually decreased throughout time, as newer copies were made of old maps. The evidence points towards the existence of an ancient maritime civilisation, thousands of years before 4000 BCE, which was the last date that Antarctica was free of ice. (For further data consult Colin Wilson, *From Atlantis to the Sphinx* and Charles Hapgood, *Maps of the Ancient Sea Kings*; see Further Reading.)

The story of Atlantis begins, from our point of view, with Plato. In *Timaeus and Critias* Plato speaks of Atlantis and its war with an antideluvian Athens. The Atlanteans were highly advanced, their capital city situated on a hill, surrounded by concentric canals and connected by tunnels large enough to accommodate a ship. Plato's detailed description makes Atlantis sound very much like its portrayal in many films – a utopia of beauty and sophistication. There is no historical evidence revealing advanced civilisation in Greece at the time indicated (i.e. 9600 BCE), although there is evidence to show that archaeology can sometimes be in error, which we shall be encountering in the following passage. Scholars are at pains to discount Plato's remarks on Atlantis. The Appendix to the Penguin edition of *Timaeus and Critias*, 1971, explains that

'Atlantis . . . is part of a middle episode in an attempt to grapple with the problems of human history and the ideal and real in human society'. In other words, it is allegory, or 'science fiction' as the Appendix later describes *Critias*. I cannot help feeling, as I read this, that some people will go to great lengths rather than accept the most simple explanation. That there did exist an advanced civilisation in the remote past that was destroyed by flood, as so many legends worldwide indicate, and that Plato was talking about something real, albeit possibly distorted by patriotism and hearsay.

Atlantis has interested many great scholars, including an American congressman Ignatius Donnelly and British Prime Minister Gladstone. Investigation of Atlantis lost its respectability when it was taken over by the occultists, starting with Helen Blavatsky, the founder of the Theosophical Society. In *Isis Unveiled* Blavatsky describes the Atlanteans as advanced, telepathic beings who became corrupt and brought themselves to destruction. It seems that some of the fascination of Atlantis lies in its fall, for we are full of unanswered questions about our own future. Similar ideas were advanced by Rudolf Steiner. The 'sleeping prophet' Edgar Cayce gave a vast body of psychic readings regarding Atlantis. Survivors of the cataclysm that destroyed Atlantis were said by Cayce to have come to the Nile Valley in the eleventh millennium BCE and there exists a large body of readings, given by the prophet, concerning this and the former lives of many who consulted him as previously incarnated Atlanteans. Cayce himself was their High Priest, Ra-Ta. Cayce gave quite specific directions concerning a repository of ancient Atlantean records in Egypt, and one reading states that a passage runs from the right paw of the Sphinx to this chamber. The Association for Research and Enlightenment, affiliated to the Edgar Cayce Foundation, has financed much serious scholarship and investigation into Egypt and the Sphinx. Indeed, seismological work undertaken by the American geophysicist Thomas Dobecki in the early 1990s did indicate the presence of a large, apparently human-made chamber beneath the Sphinx.

There have been many other theories about the Lost Continent. A later theory suggests that 'Atlantis' was actually the island of Santorini, north of Crete, and this theory has achieved some popularity, even though Plato states that Atlantis was beyond the Pillars of Hercules (i.e. the Straits of Gibraltar). In spite of scholarly derision, the idea of Atlantis persists. In respect of a Lost Continent, which does not have to have been precisely in the Atlantic, it seems to me there is no smoke without fire and that somewhere in the story may lie clues to the 'open secret' that I sense. Perhaps to the Atlanteans, this was no 'secret' at all.

EGYPTIAN MYSTERIES

The Sphinx and the pyramids fill me with awe and a sense of – something. I just don't accept accounts of pharaonic tombs, of thousands of slaves toiling in the desert sun to hoist vast slabs of stone, of primitive rites and superstitious beliefs ignorant by comparison with our own. The monuments of megalomaniac tyrants are left like Shelley's 'Ozymandias' a 'colossal wreck' around which 'The lone and level sands stretch far away'. The pyramids simply do not strike me that way. One only has to look at photographs of the Giza plateau to get the idea that here is a majestic mystery. Something was going on here that we do not understand and, perhaps, in a sense it is still 'going on'.

Egypt houses many enigmas. Despite various theories, we do not know how the pyramids were built, nor could we build a similar structure even with modern technology. The interior structure of the pyramids, notably the Great

Pyramid, makes no sense at all, with passages and chambers constructed with minute accuracy and unbelievable engineering skill, leading ... nowhere. I simply do not feel that we are sufficiently humble in the face of these facts. Archaeologists insist that certain things are known about ancient Egypt. It seems to me that we 'know' almost nothing that is relevant and that we could fruitfully go back to basics, approaching the question with the simplicity of a child, for we may be children in the face of the knowledge of those who built the pyramids.

The Sphinx is, if anything, more of a puzzle. Robert Bauval (see Further Reading) says of this monument '... nothing else that has reached us from antiquity even remotely matches its power and grandeur, its majesty and its mystery, or its sombre and hypnotic watchfulness'. He

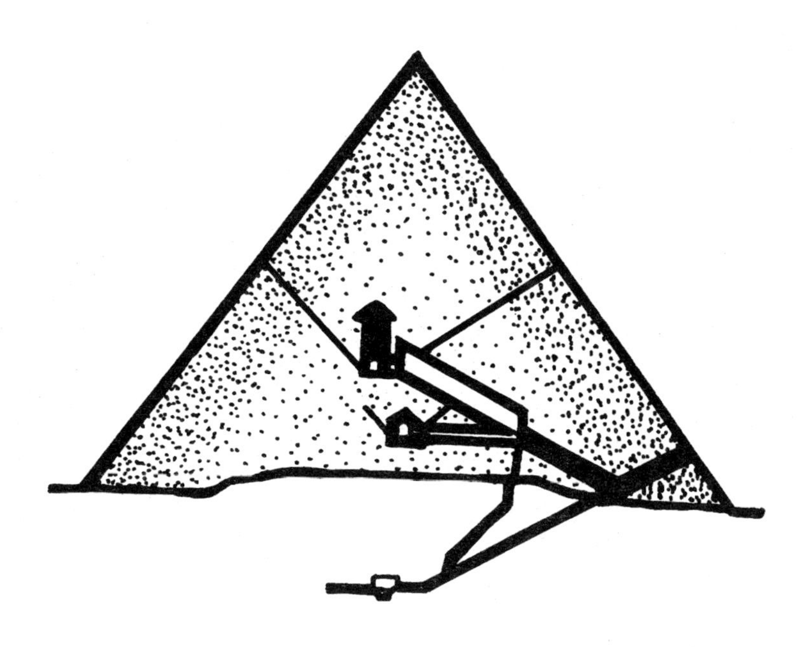

Cross-section through the Great Pyramid

continues, 'In all honesty ... what confronts us at Giza is an entirely anonymous monument, carved out of undatable rock, about which, as the forthright Egyptologist Selim Hassan wrote ... "no definite facts are known".' Modern scholars insist that the Sphinx was built by the Pharaoh Khafre (Greek name Chepren) but this is on the basis of a single syllable carved on the granite stella between the paws of the Sphinx, that may or may not be the first part of Khafre's name. We shall return later to the Sphinx, but for now let us mark the fact that this enormous creature of stone is unidentified and unexplained. We know neither who built it, nor when, nor do we know why, or how.

The pyramids present us with many well-known puzzles. For instance, the stones used to build them are chiselled with an unbelievable precision so that the mean variation on the cutting of the stone from a straight line and from a true square is only 0.025 cm (0.01 inch) per length of 190 cm (75 inches) up the face, as observed by Sir Flinders Petrie. Again, although the figure pi, 3.1416, representing the ratio of the diameter of a circle to its circumference is believed not to have been discovered until the Greeks did so, in the third century BCE, yet the designed height of the Great Pyramid, 146.729 metres (481.3949 feet) – has the same relationship to the perimeter of its base, which is 921.459 metres (3023.16 feet), as the circumference of a circle to its radius (i.e. 2 pi). That is 146.729 m (481.3949 feet) × 2 × 3.14 (taking the shortened form of pi, which is a recurring decimal) = 921.459 m (3023.16 feet). The proportions of the pyramid also have a relationship to the earth at exactly 1:43,200. This means, in practice, that if you multiply the height by 43,200 you get a quotient of 6338.693 km (3938.685 miles), just 18 km (11 miles) less than the true polar radius of the earth as we calculate it today. The perimeter treated similarly comes to within 275 km (170 miles) of the equatorial circumference of the earth, an error of only three-quarters of a per cent. It is well known that the pyramid is aligned to the cardinal points, and this has been accomplished with amazing precision, the average deviation from true amounting to only 5 per cent of one degree. The Great Pyramid is located at almost exactly one-third of the distance between the North Pole and the equator, hardly a mile to the south of latitude 30. In addition, the basic pyramid shape has been shown to possess unexplained powers, such as the ability to preserve organic matter and to sharpen razor blades, as well as affect the moods and health of people inside a pyramid structure. The proportions quoted above are just some of the incredibly precise measurements to which the pyramid was built. Unless the Egyptians were afflicted, as a race, with obsessive–compulsive neurosis there must have been a good reason for this. We don't know what this was, any more than we know how it was wrought.

In addition to the accepted ancient Egyptian riddles, there are others that are simply ignored by conventional Egyptologists. In 1893, the archaeologist, Flinders Petrie, found vases in the village of Neqada, 480 km (300 miles) to the south of Cairo. They bore none of the marks consistent with the potter's wheel, but were too perfect to be made by hand. Assuming they must date from 2000 BCE, Petrie named their creators 'the New Race'. Subsequently, similar vases were found in tombs dating from 1,000 years earlier. Because these vases no longer fitted the chronology – it was stretching a point to believe they could have been made by a primitive culture in the first place – Petrie adopted the admirable expedient of dropping the vases from his records. This scenario, of ignoring the inexplicable, unacceptable or disconcerting, is not rare; I call it 'the ostrich syndrome'. However, Petrie, whom Robert Bauval and Graham Hancock describe as 'one of the oddball giants of Egyptology' by no means discarded all anomalies. For instance, his opinion on a piece of iron found in the air-passage shaft of the Great Pyramid in 1837 was that it was,

indeed, very ancient, that is from well before the so-called 'Iron Age'. This was confirmed in 1989 by experienced metallurgists Dr M.P. Jones and Dr Sayed El Gayer, who stated the piece was certainly ancient, and human-made, and that there was evidence that this had been incorporated into the structure of the Great Pyramid when it was built. Their findings were ignored by the British Museum.

To return to the evidence of vases, examples with necks too narrow even to admit a little finger have been unearthed, such that we could not reproduce today. In another context, close examination of holes drilled into a rock composed of quartz and feldspar revealed that the drill had cut through the quartz faster than the feldspar, although the quartz is harder. Modern ultrasonic machines use vibration and quartz crystals respond to this. Christopher Dunn, a modern toolmaker cited by Colin Wilson, suggests that the Egyptians had some sort of force based on sound, so reinforcing the statements made by David Elkington. If this is so, a technology vastly in advance of ours, possessed by a society that simply thought differently from us, is suggested. These may have been people who were able to think more holistically, more totally, to connect knowledge, ideas, practices from what we would regard as separate disciplines and to create from this something that was greater than the sum of its parts. To adapt a familiar analogy, they were able to hover over the wood, discerning all the trees and the wood as a totality, in addition to how the wood fitted in to the surrounding countryside. By contrast, we are lost in contemplation of bits of bark, hardly even wondering where the horizon is. There is no specific indication for this advanced and panoramic consciousness. It is an impression created by a combination of evidence for high-precision engineering, advanced technology, suggestion of ancient wisdom and concealed records and the many links that construction on the Giza plateau appears to bear to the earth and the heavens. Make of it what you will.

AS ABOVE, SO BELOW

Robert Bauval (see Further Reading) has put forward the theory that the whole Giza necropolis was built to mirror the heavens, with the three pyramids laid out to represent the three stars on the 'belt' of the constellation of Orion, while the Nile represents the band of the Milky Way. For the ancient Egyptians, Orion was an important constellation, believed to be the home of Osiris, god of the dead.

The shafts in the Great Pyramid, known as 'air shafts', targeted the meridian transits of several important stars, as they were placed in the third century BCE. From the Queen's Chamber, Beta Ursa Minor and Sirius, the star associated with the great goddess Isis, consort to Osiris and mother of Horus, were singled out. Sirius is an especially important star which appears to defy precession. (For an explanation of precession, please see Chapter 2.) All stars have their own motion, called 'proper motion' and, because of the proximity of Sirius to our own solar system and the speed and direction of its proper motion, its heliacal rising heralded the flooding of the Nile for 3,000 years. Shafts from the King's Chamber targeted Alpha Draconis and Zeta Orionis, the brightest and lowest of the three stars in Orion's belt. All of these stars were important in Egyptian mythology. It seems that the Great Pyramid was no tomb but a building planned for important ritual, possibly to send the soul of the deceased straight on its way to Zeta Orionis, to reign forever with Osiris.

However, the three pyramids, while they may be aligned in a similar fashion to the three stars of Orion's belt, are actually twisted in relation to the position of Orion, as it now appears in the sky. The only time when these three stars were *actually* reflected in the pyramids was 10,500 BCE, when Orion, due to the movement of precession, was close to the horizon and tilted at an angle that is, indeed, mirrored in these three pyramids. All these stellar positions have been proved by computer simulation of the skies of ancient Egypt. There is too much here for coincidence.

For another dramatic point let us return to the Sphinx. Conventional history indicates that the Sphinx was built around 2500 BCE by the pharaoh Chepren. However, recent studies have shown that the Sphinx has been eroded by water, not sand. Robert Schoch, a geologist from Boston University in the United States, has verified this, estimating the building of the Sphinx to have taken place at around 7000 BCE, when the Sahara was still a fertile area upon which rain fell. The Sphinx is more weathered than Old Kingdom tombs nearby, which means it is older. Further than this, the Sphinx temples contain blocks larger than any found in the Great Pyramid. From this, we could justifiably contend that the builders of the Sphinx were much more advanced than those who came later, indicating a society of immense technical ability, whose knowledge later decayed. This goes against all we believe about 'advancement' where a steady progression up the ladder of achievement is visualised through history. However, is there any reason why this should not happen? Imagine trying to explain the internal combustion engine to primitive tribespeople and then leaving them to make their own car. One or two of them with an aptitude for engineering might be able to understand and construct the vehicle, assuming the materials were to hand, but we can imagine the passing on of the expertise might resemble Chinese whispers, with the result, after several generations, being almost unrecognisable as an automobile. It seems reasonable to postulate that in the dim and distant past there may indeed have been a civilisation far more advanced than we can imagine and that this civilisation passed on its knowledge to the Egyptians, the Mayans and others. These are our Atlanteans, by any other name.

According to Bauval, the accumulation of evidence points to a highly advanced civilisation that built the Sphinx in approximately 10,500 BCE. The final, dramatic point is that an observer, standing between the feline paws of the Sphinx at the spring equinox of the year 10,500 BCE would see the constellation of Leo rising over the horizon just before the solar disk. This would have constituted the start of the Age of Leo, mentioned in Chapter 2, the Golden Age of 'Zep Tepi' or the Egyptian First Time. Astrologers will note that the sun rules Leo – was this a time of glory, when the gods walked the earth? Turning from the rising sun and looking exactly south, the constellation of Orion appears, reflecting in the starry sky the layout of the pyramids on the ground. The leonine shape of the Sphinx, the indications of its age deduced from patterns of weathering and the many myths of Atlanteans all point to a time of around 10,500 BCE. These 'Atlanteans' possessed extremely sophisticated knowledge of astronomy. Their civilisation destroyed by catastrophe, they marked the start of the new Age of Leo, as we now mark the Age of Aquarius, except that they built enduring markers for posterity. However, the pyramids, although planned when the sphinx was built, were actually constructed at a much later time, and here Bauval and Hancock are in agreement with convention, setting the date at about 2500 BCE. By this time, the constellation of Orion (i.e. the god Osiris) had drifted up the bank of the celestial Nile, which was the Milky Way, until its position coincided with the land of the Sphinx, on earth. Now the god was truly revitalised, able to take up his rightful home in the sky, as resurrected lord.

This would have been a tremendous climax in the religious life of the Egyptians. If we are correct that they lived their spiritual beliefs continually and vividly, in contrast to our own compartmentalised observances, then this event, culmination of thousands of years of preparation and expectation, must have been almost unimaginably

momentous. The myth of Osiris tells of his murder and dismemberment at the hands of his evil brother, Set, his magical reconstitution and revivication by his grieving wife, Isis, long enough to conceive his son, Horus, who then avenges him. Osiris reigns as King of the Underworld, or abode of the dead, which may have been in the skies, rather than below the ground. His 'rebirth' must have been akin to a second coming. More than this, it heralded immortality for the Pharaoh and his people. If this is true, it would have been far more than a superstitious belief, but an act of true and vast magical significance, in the sense that magic is a transformation of consciousness. By this union with their skies the Egyptians would have found deep significance in their lives that is not adequately explained by the modern outlook of 'A causes B, Orion causes immortality'. Basically, it would surely have been a massive statement of 'oneness', the import of which we cannot totally imagine. There may also be specific information encoded in the layout of the Giza plateau, targeted at our age, as we acquire the sophistication to decipher what we see. As we stand on the threshold of the Aquarian Age, as the ancient priests apparently stood on the threshold of the Age of Leo, perhaps we can share something of their vision of cosmic cycles, and our place in them.

VIBRATIONS

Here we leave the realms of academic hinterland and mythology to explore even stranger lands. It is time for all of us 'space cadets' to fasten our seat belts for a ride into the speculative. Much of the following is drawn from Bob Frissell's book *Nothing In This Book Is True, But It's Exactly How Things Are*. I believe the book bears this strange title not because it is some kind of send-up but because it seeks to reveal a reality that is not 'reality' as we know it, taking the myths concerning ancient Egypt and Atlantis much further. By all means be sceptical, for scepticism is healthy, but do not close your mind.

In several places in this book we have explored the notions of other dimensions and expansion of consciousness without being quite clear exactly what these may mean. Bob Frissell sets this out explicitly, so offering a possibly valuable piece for my 'open secret' jigsaw. He states there are, indeed, different dimensions, that the only difference between dimensional worlds is their wavelength, that wavelength is the key to the universe, that our reality is created by wavelength alone and that the wavelength of our third-dimensional world is 7.23 cm (2.85 inches). He goes on to explain that the different dimensions are separated in relation to each other in the same way that notes are separated on a musical scale. The octave on a piano is made up from eight white keys and five black keys, making thirteen in all, the thirteenth actually being the first note of the following octave.

> *In between each note and the next are twelve harmonic, holographic points; in dimensional terms these are the overtones. It is also the same as changing channels on a TV set. When you operate the channel control, you are tuning to different wavelengths.*
>
> *There is a voidness between dimensions like the voidness between two notes. There is a greater void, a great wall if you will, between octaves. Each dimension is also separated from the others by a 90-degree rotation. If you could change wavelengths and rotate 90 degrees you would disappear from this world and reappear in whatever dimension you were tuned to . . . .*
>
> *For example, if we were to go up one level, which we are in the process of doing, we would find that whatever we think, as soon as we think it, instantly manifests. Here, by contrast, on the third dimension,*

> *there is a time delay. Even though our thoughts create our reality unerringly here as well, their manifestation is obviously not instant.*

These remarks about the musical scale echo what we discussed earlier, about the power of sound.

As an aside, I should like to explain here that the key to creating a good and loving 'reality' is not by the repression of bad thoughts and 'making wrong' but by fully experiencing and living through emotions so that we may be transformed by them, for what is resisted not only persists but grows stronger. In his book, Frissell gives instructions for experiencing, breathing and relaxing that can help to make a shift, but it is outside our scope to examine this in this book.

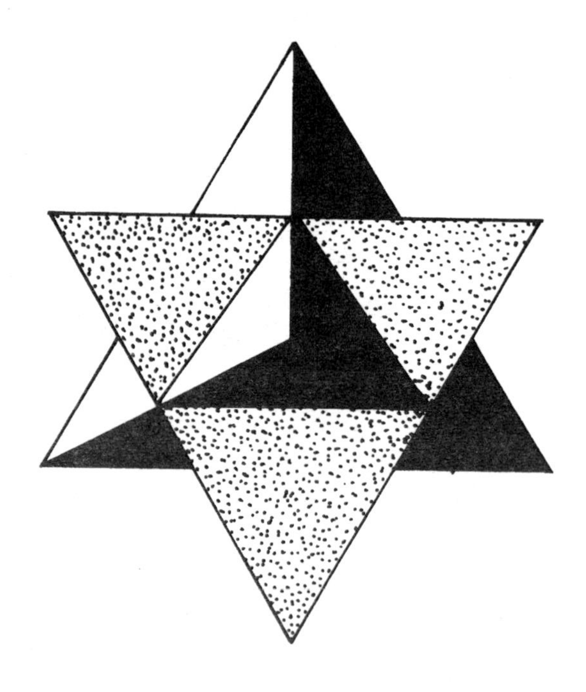

A star tetrahedron

GEOMETRY

How do we achieve this move from one dimension to another? Frissell describes an electromagnetic field, called the merkaba, that surrounds the body of each person and, in fact, every thing. The shape of the merkaba is that of a star tetrahedron. The apexes of the star tetrahedron are connected by a tube running through the body. Learning the method of breathing through this tube along with rotating energy fields produces the merkaba which is a vehicle of ascension.

> *We have a physical body, a mental body, and an emotional body and they all have star tetrahedronal shapes. These are three identical fields superimposed over each other, the only difference among them being that the physical body alone is locked – it does not rotate. The merkaba is created by counter-rotating fields of energy. The mental star tetrahedronal field is electrical in nature, male, and rotates to the left. The emotional star tetrahedronal field is magnetic in nature, female, and rotates to the right.* It is the linking together of the mind, heart, and physical body *(my emphasis) in a specific geometrical ratio and at a critical speed that produces the merkaba ....*
>
> *... the counter-rotating fields of light of the merkaba comprise a time–space vehicle. Once you know how to activate these fields you can use your merkaba to travel throughout the universe.*

It is sacred geometry that underlies all of life, forming the morphogenetic structure behind reality. Rupert Sheldrake, the biologist, is known for his theory of morphogenetic fields, put forward in the Hypothesis of Formative Causation. This field exists behind physical form, as a non-physical template containing information outside of the physical brain through which an individual has access to the

species memory through 'morphic resonance' – thus a chicken 'knows' how to become an egg. This seems to me to be a scientific way of talking about what is, essentially, spirit. Frissell states that the essence of this field is geometric. Scientists, in fact, now confirm that the movements of particles subsequent to the Big Bang were geometrical in pattern, not haphazard. According to Frissell and others, the penultimate pattern behind creation is the flower of life, through which has been wrought all that

The flower of life

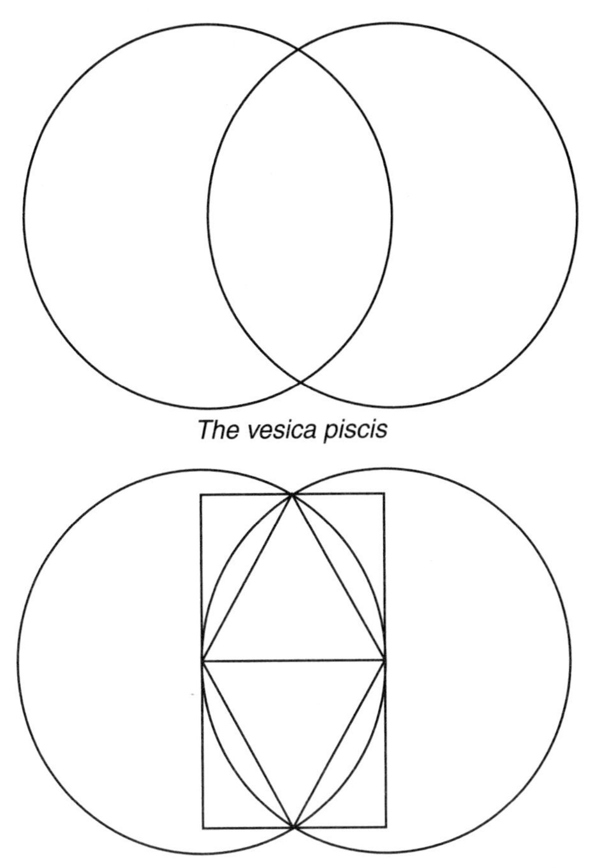

The vesica piscis

The vesica piscis, showing how two equilateral triangles fit inside, and two squares, forming a rectangle, fit around

exists. The flower of life is depicted in one of the oldest temples in Egypt – Frissell does not specify which. The flower of life is composed of the vesica piscis, a shape which underlies certain ancient structures in England, such as Castlerigg stone circle, in Northumbria, and it is found on the lid of Chalice Well, a centre for pilgrimage in Glastonbury, Somerset. It is taken to represent the vulva of

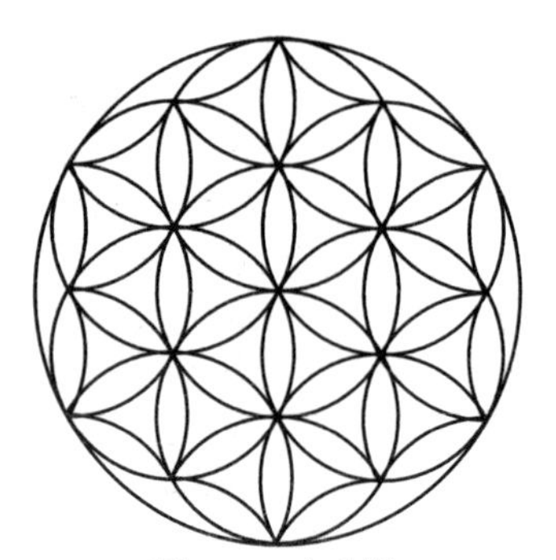

The seed of life

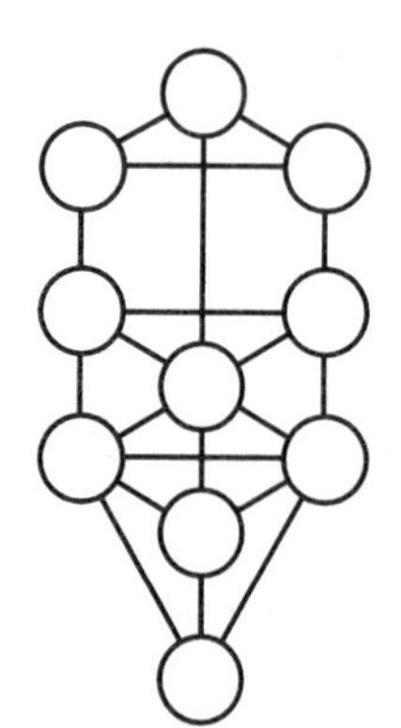

The tree of life

Showing how the tree of life fits over the seed of life

the Goddess. From the vesica piscis can be generated the hexagram, which looks like a two-dimensional star tetrahedron. By playing with geometry it is possible to see how one shape is generated by another, fits into it, expands upon it and so forth. Sacred geometry is flawless and it has often been stated that secrets of geometry were encoded in ancient structures, from Stonehenge to Chartres Cathedral. The hidden language may have been acquired (or re-acquired) from the Middle East by the Knights Templar, and was passed down through generations of masons, who left their messages encrypted in the stonework. A Gothic cathedral resonates to certain sounds in such a way as to produce potential peak experience, bringing together the elements of sound (i.e. vibration and shape). (To explore this further you may like to start with *Earth Mysteries – A Beginner's Guide*; see Further Reading.)

Frissell goes on to explain how spirit projects itself to form creation. This is paralleled by passages from the book of Genesis, but I take it to refer not merely to the creation of the universe but to the start of anything, in the way that the Qabalistic Tree of Life (which is contained within the seed and the flower of life) is a diagram of manifestation of any process, entity or situation from spirit into matter. In other words, creation is constant, not consigned to some remote point in antiquity. Spirit first projected itself in six directions, then linked four of the points so created to form a square, then a pyramid, then an octahedron. Following this, curved lines come into play because creation is smoother and easier from curves. Curves are considered female, straight lines males, hence the story that the female was created after the male. Through these curves, the flower of life blossoms into creation. The ratios and patterns so generated underlie all of the manifest universe and knowledge of this is necessary in order to progress effectively.

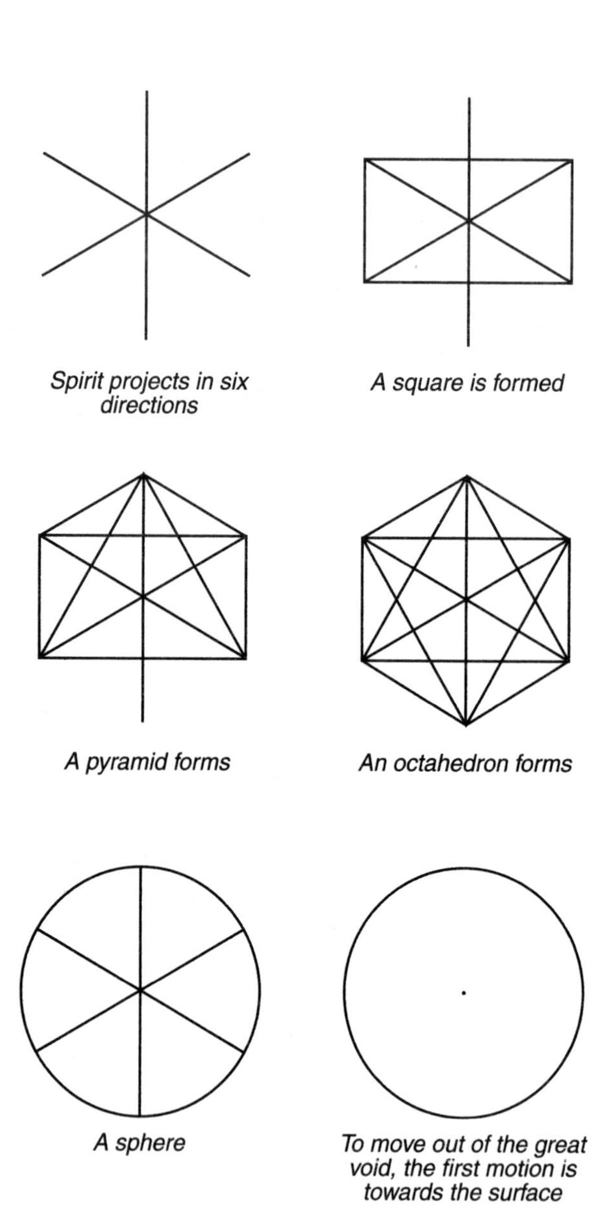

Projection of spirit in six directions

The following is, I think, a most important point. The understanding of geometry is the method for integrating the functions of the left and right brain. Those of us involved in the intuitive arts and esoteric subjects are usually aware of a sneering dismissive voice that says 'naaa – get away' when we try to put our insights into practice, or to develop them. This is the logical, analytical left brain that cuts into our finely woven tapestry of the imagination, leaving us divided and conquered. As another instance, I often wonder if the complex symbology of astrology is a way of keeping the left brain 'quiet' while the intuition does its stuff! The science of geometry convinces our left brain that there is spirit behind all and, once convinced, integration begins to take place and we move from polarity into unity consciousness.

We have space only for a taster of this description of the workings of sacred geometry, but I feel intuitively that it has something to do with the overall picture that I have been seeking. I have never liked geometry or mathematics as taught in schools and found most of it dry and incomprehensible, but geometry described like this is intriguing. Here, we have not just a set of rules and measurements, but something that impinges upon the eternal. If you want to know more, consult Bob Frissell's book or look out for Flower of Life workshops in your area. At the time of writing I know these to be available in England and the United States. Failing this, information can be obtained by writing straight to Bob Frissell, c/o North Atlantic Books, PO Box 12327, Berkeley, CA 94712, USA.

ANOTHER HISTORY

While historians sneer and adventurous scholars venture tentative suggestions, there are many people who take the former existence of a Lost Continent as read and, furthermore, that this was connected with visitors from other planets and star systems who were and are closely involved in our development. Many people refuse to take any of this seriously. Personally, I find ideas of value here. Here is an alternative history. Please hold on to your space helmets.

Frissell points out that, 'In order for us to understand what is happening now and what will happen in our future, it is essential that we know the past.' This is highly relevant for us, standing as we do on the threshold of a new millennium, and asking many questions about the meanings of our lives. We have encountered some instances of evidence from the past that has been ignored by conventional scholars because they don't fit in, and this is but a tip of the iceberg. To challenge the accepted view is considered heresy and the image of the dispassionate scientist seeking truth is largely a mirage. For many other instances of how inconvenient facts have been left out of the picture, I refer again to the many examples quoted by Colin Wilson in *From Atlantis to the Sphinx* (see Further Reading), especially the chapters on 'Forbidden Archaeology'. If we are to get a clear perspective on ourselves we must surely transcend academic dogma as well as religious dogma.

Frissell continues, 'As humans we have to know our history because we have to know how we got into our present predicament in order to get out of it.' Much of our accepted history is depressingly fatalistic. For instance, Darwin's theory of the survival of the fittest seems to raise the inevitability of conflict and destruction, as the strong wipe out the weak, and always, in the end, succeed. Life began as an accident and evolved through competition. Now we have reached the point where our competence in conquering each other and the environment stands to wipe us out. Being the creatures we are, this seems inevitable, and to cherish a more hopeful view can be dismissed as

Utopian. So why not carry on patting ourselves on the back for being Top Nation of the Top Species and continue our ravenous consumerism, and at least enjoy ourselves as much as we can, while we can? But surely there must be more to life . . . ?

Alternative 'history' states that civilisation on this planet goes back 500,000,000 years and there have been civilisations so far in advance of ours that we cannot possibly imagine them. Many life-forms have come here, interbred, formed new species and departed, and each life-form must evolve through five levels of consciousness. Our present position is on the second of the five levels. There are many anecdotes from indigenous peoples stating that we have been visited from the stars.

One of the most well-known such anecdotes concerns the Dogon tribe, who live in Africa, close to Timbuktu, who have known things about the star Sirius for centuries, and these facts have only recently been discovered by astronomers. The Dogon knew that Sirius is a double star, with a tiny star rotating around the larger body, composed of the heaviest matter in creation, and that this star was very old and had a revolution period of 50 years. Now we know that a white dwarf, Sirius B, does go round Sirius A, and that its period is 50.1 years. Stan Gooch, in *Cities of Dreams* (Aulis, 1995) attributes such knowledge to a tradition passed on from the Neanderthal, who, he says, in fact had an awesome, intuitive civilisation, in which astronomy played an important part. Such information as the Dogon possessed could have been passed down verbally from Neanderthal time (Gooch makes the valid point that information certainly was passed accurately, by word of mouth, down thousands of years, so why not 30,000 years?). However, the Dogon also possess extensive knowledge of the solar system, including the moons of other planets (see Robert Temple, *The Sirius Mystery*, Sidgwick & Jackson, 1976). Again, we have a suggestion of

ancient, lost, highly advanced civilisations. Gooch's theories about the Neanderthal are thought provoking. Neanderthal had a much larger brain than us and it must surely be possible that there was a Neanderthal civilisation that was overthrown by and – as Gooch believes – interbred with, by Cro-Magnon humans. However, it seems unlikely that our lost civilisation/s were simply Neanderthal. The Dogon also tell a story about the landing of a spacecraft from Sirius, from which creatures emerged who made a large hole in the ground which they filled with water. Then they jumped into the water and came to the shore and communed with the Dogon, telling them they were from Sirius. Despite the fact that the Dogon possess highly accurate information about Sirius, this story is dismissed as simply myth.

Speculation exists concerning a tenth planet in our solar system, which we have already encountered in Chapter 3. 'Alternative history' states that the beings from this planet, called the Nefilim, came to earth 400,000 years ago, to mine gold which they needed to maintain their atmosphere. The Nefilim made contact with the dolphins initially, for these were on a similar level of consciousness. The most advanced life-forms do not manipulate their external environment for they create internally all that they need. The most intelligent, oldest and advanced life on earth is the whales, next come the dolphins and then humans. Whales have been here alive and conscious for 500,000,000 years and they hold the memory of the planet – an idea upon which one of my favourite films, *Star Trek IV*, was based. This is science fiction, of course, but science fiction is not always just a story, for it can also be an intuitive vision of what will transpire, or has transpired, in some form or fashion.

The Nefilim joined with the Sirians to make us. We were created to mine their gold, but I believe there was more to this than the simple generation of a servant species, for the

Nefilim had to get permission and co-operation on other dimensional levels. Seven of the Nefilim exited from their bodies to form a sphere of consciousness which was, in effect, an ovum. From this a cool flame appeared that was set in the Halls of Amenti, an ancient place existing from before 5,500,000 years ago. The Halls of Amenti do not exist in this dimension, but in a space-warp that resembles a womb, sitting a dimensional overtone higher than earth. In respect of the geographical earth, the Halls of Amenti are not always in the same place. At the time of Atlantis they were on the surface, they have been out in space but now they are below the earth's crust. Beings from a planet in orbit around Sirius B now also came and entered the flame in the Halls of Amenti. In this way, our race was created, but because we were hybrids, like mules, we could not reproduce. However, we ate the 'fruit of a tree' forbidden by the Nefilim, and through its effects gained the ability to reproduce ourselves. Now we were out of the control of the Nefilim and due to their displeasure we were thrown out of their special 'garden'. I am sure you recognise this story! None the less, we were able to grow food and progress, until there occurred a shift in the earth's poles. Such a shift, in addition to causing massive damage, also causes the collective memory to be lost because this is dependent upon the magnetic field of the earth. Pole shift is connected with a shift in consciousness. This shift threw up the lost continent of Lemuria, to which the survivors escaped.

Lemurian technology worked with the mind and the heart linked together. This civilisation was predominantly 'feminine' and intuitive. The Lemurians learned the art of Ascension, which means the ability to raise consciously through the dimensional levels, taking your body with you. The Lemurians knew their land was sinking and migrated to other parts of the globe. Another pole shift took place. Lemuria sank and Atlantis emerged. This brings us to roughly 80,000 years ago. Certain immortal masters went to Atlantis and created a system of energy vortices based on the ten sephiroth of the Tree of Life, that drew other Lemurians to the vortex to which each individual was compatible. However, the Lemurian civilisation had developed consciousness of only eight of the ten vortices upon the Tree of Life. Study of the Tree of Life involves study of the Qabalah, in order that a fuller understanding may be attained. For now, suffice to say that the Tree of Life is a kind of blueprint of creation and its stages, starting with pure energy and emerging into physical form. Each of the sephiroth, that is each of the 'globes' or centres of energy upon the tree when it is drawn, called 'sephiroth' (singular *sephira*), possess a specific characteristic or vibration, and each have their special place in the scheme of things. As we have seen, this is part of the sacred geometry that lies beneath existence. Leaving two sephiroth undeveloped does not mean that they do not exist, but merely that they have not been consciously formed. Lemurian society had not adapted to these two sephiroth, thus these centres were left empty, yet activated. Into these two empty spaces came aliens.

EXTRA-TERRESTRIALS

Two uninvited extra-terrestrials were drawn into these two spaces, and then became part of our evolutionary pattern. One of these were the Hebrews, whose origin was unknown, and they did not cause any problem. In fact, they helped because they brought advanced information. The others were a different kettle of fish entirely, because they were Martians, although not from Mars as we know it, or even the Mars that existed then, but rather the Mars that existed a million years ago, when the planet was beautiful and vibrant. However, Mars had a massive problem, because the Martians had evolved a method for creating the merkaba externally, that is synthetically, without love and without the involvement of the feeling nature. Ultimately, this is unimaginably destructive because it creates duality, destroying perception of the One Spirit and creating a race of creatures who cannot feel. The Greys, whom we met in Chapter 3, are descendants of these Martians, a species who has lost its ability to feel and to procreate and is thus dying.

Mars at this time was a highly developed left-brain culture and the Martians' self-centred attitude was destroying their planet much in the way we are destroying our planet at present. Certain of these calculating and warlike creatures built their own external merkaba, a time–space vehicle, a precise and highly complex mathematical structure in the humanoid face area on Mars photographed by the Viking spacecraft in 1976, called Cydonia. They got in it and left for Atlantis, which was far into their future but about 65,000 years in our past. As Frissell puts it:

> *When the Martians stepped into our evolutionary pattern in Atlantis we were about the equivalent of a thirteen or fourteen-year-old girl and they were the equivalent of a sixty-five-year-old man. They stepped into our evolutionary pattern against our will and, essentially, raped us . . . they would have taken over if they could have, but there weren't enough of them so they had to go along with our ingenue program at least for a while.*

For some 50,000 years, little took place and earth retained much of its female orientation, although there was significant distortion towards the Masculine. Then 16,000 years ago a great comet hit our planet in the area of South Carolina. Despite having the ability to shoot the comet out of the sky the instinctual go-with-the-flow 'Feminine' orientation prevailed and the comet was allowed to fall. As it happens, instinct had, in certain respects, been wise, for the comet landed where the bulk of the Martians were

living. However, for those that remained it was the last straw and they decided to resume their soulless, technological quest. They created an external merkaba and everything went badly wrong, for this vehicle ripped through the dimensions drawing many entities here that were bewildered and lost. The remains of this failed experiment are on the ocean floor in the area of the well-known Bermuda triangle, where ships and planes have inexplicably disappeared. The Bermuda triangle is a triangular tip of part of the synthetic merkaba field, that is quite out of control. This venture sent everything and everybody crazy (in fact, we are still suffering from the effects of this inter-dimensional rift). At this point, the ascended masters stepped in and healed the rift, but things were still bad and for 4,000 years they kept getting worse. The true path of life dictates that the Martians and the disembodied entities could not be destroyed, for at the level of unity consciousness a loss for one is a loss for all. Thus, a process was evolved to raise the consciousness of the entire planet to unity, or Christ-consciousness, to create a situation where all would be healed. This involves creating a synthetic Christ-consciousness grid on the planet, so the process of evolution is greatly speeded up.

LEVELS OF CONSCIOUSNESS

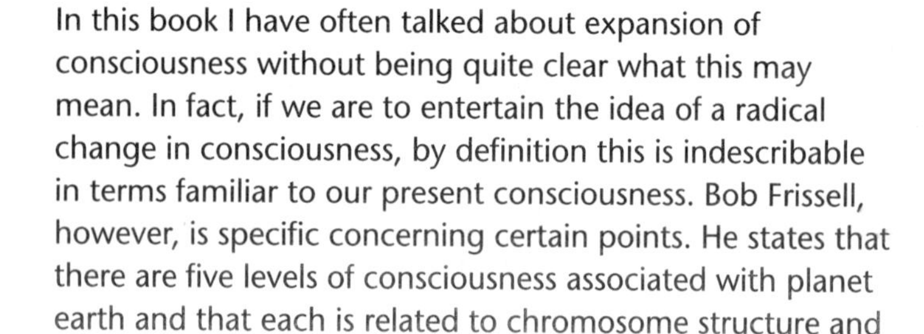

In this book I have often talked about expansion of consciousness without being quite clear what this may mean. In fact, if we are to entertain the idea of a radical change in consciousness, by definition this is indescribable in terms familiar to our present consciousness. Bob Frissell, however, is specific concerning certain points. He states that there are five levels of consciousness associated with planet earth and that each is related to chromosome structure and to stature.

- The **first level** has 42 plus 2 chromosomes and is associated with a height range of 1 metre (3.5 feet) to 1.5 metres (5 feet) in height. Collective consciousness prevails at this level and it corresponds to the Dreamtime of the Aborigines and the feeling of primitive unity that I have described elsewhere as something we need to retrieve, only *consciously*.
- The **second level** has 44 plus 2 chromosomes and is our present level, with a height range of 1.5 metres (5 feet) to 2 metres (6.5 feet).
- The **third level** is Christ consciousness. This seems to me to correspond with the next stage I visualise for humankind, where there is both consciousness of Self and consciousness of All, where the Dreamtime state is retained yet with a level of sharpness and with the retaining of the discriminative faculty. Frissell calls this 'no longer dreamtime but realtime'. Here there exists unity memory along with instant manifestation, where what is thought, or remembered becomes instantly real, as it is part of the memory of every Christ-consciousness being that ever existed. This level has 46 plus 2 chromosomes and is associated with a height range of 3 metres (10 feet) to 5 metres (16 feet)
- The **fourth level** is, again, disharmonic, like our own, but also like our own it is a necessary step in order to progress to the fifth level. This level has 48 plus 2 chromosomes and is associated with a height range of 7.5 metres (25 feet) to 10.5 metres (35 feet).
- The **fifth level** is the highest achievable on this planet. This level is associated with 50 plus 2 chromosomes and a height range of 15 metres (50 feet) to 18 metres (60 feet). So it seems that giants did once walk the earth, and possibly will again.

THOTH AND THE PYRAMIDS

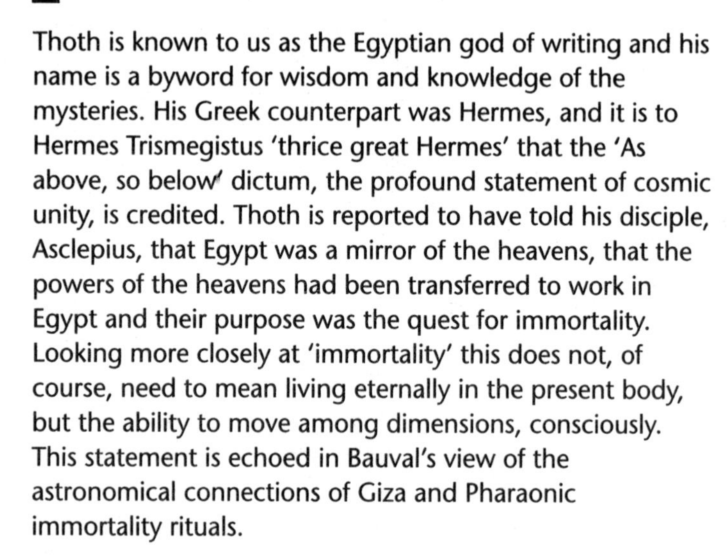

Thoth is known to us as the Egyptian god of writing and his name is a byword for wisdom and knowledge of the mysteries. His Greek counterpart was Hermes, and it is to Hermes Trismegistus 'thrice great Hermes' that the 'As above, so below' dictum, the profound statement of cosmic unity, is credited. Thoth is reported to have told his disciple, Asclepius, that Egypt was a mirror of the heavens, that the powers of the heavens had been transferred to work in Egypt and their purpose was the quest for immortality. Looking more closely at 'immortality' this does not, of course, need to mean living eternally in the present body, but the ability to move among dimensions, consciously. This statement is echoed in Bauval's view of the astronomical connections of Giza and Pharaonic immortality rituals.

According to Bob Frissell and others, Thoth is an actual person who was king of Atlantis for 16,000 years. Thoth is an ascended master who elected to stay and help the evolution of earth, rather in the Eastern tradition of the Bodhisattva who attains consciousness of the Divine yet remains to help those left on earth. Thoth vowed to remain until we attained a certain level of consciousness and when this happened, in 1991, he left. A change came over the planet in the wake of the Gulf War, since when the forces of light have been stronger than those of darkness – the first time for many thousands of years.

Together with Ra and Araaragot, who were also former Atlantean kings, Thoth set down the blueprint for Christ-consciousness. They went to Egypt, because here was the axis point for the flame which contains the ovum of our collective consciousness. This axis comes out in Egypt and also at the other side of the earth in Moorea, creating a spiral of energy, the shadow of which, formed on the ground, looks like a logarithmic spiral. On this spiral was built three pyramids, the primary purpose of which was to take consciousness to the next level, in other words to lift a 44-plus-2 chromosome individual into Christ-consciousness and to stabilise them. These pyramids were built with mind and heart at the fourth-dimensional level, constructed from the top downwards, in a period of three days. Deep below the pyramids was made a small temple city to accommodate about 10,000 people which is still there.

Subsequently, the trio sited 83,000 sacred sites around the planet, on the fourth-dimensional level (so these are not visible to ordinary sight). This exercise was all part of the construction of the Christ-consciousness planetary grid. Every life-form has a consciousness grid in existence around the planet. I visualise this as a kind of etheric web of energy. For humans, there are three grids now in operation, the first one for the 42-plus-2 chromosome level, the second for 44-plus-2, that is the present level and, as of 4 February 1989, a third grid for the Christ-consciousness level. Bob Frissell is quite specific about the date. I cannot confirm any of this except that I and many others sense this grid. One friend of mine, who is a shamanic teacher, actually sees it and has been puzzled about its exact meaning, for it appears specifically as a criss-cross of lines. This grid has been many thousands of years in the making.

The complex in Egypt was built about 200 years before the great Deluge, told of in so many mythologies, including the biblical Flood of Noah. At this time the earth's axis shifted. Atlantis was lost and the earth descended to a lower vibrational level, which is why no evidence can be found. We are simply looking at the wrong level. Thoth went to the Sphinx, which marks the oldest object on the planet – a large spacecraft situated one mile below the surface. This is part of our protection, because at times of pole shift we are vulnerable to an influx of dark powers while the magnetic field of the planet collapses. Each time this happens, a person who has ascended to Christ-consciousness raises the ship and what they think and feel happens instantaneously. The 'spaceship' we are talking about is usually one overtone higher, vibrationally, than the earth, which is why it is able to exist underground and, although it is several hundred metres across it is only five atoms thick and actually runs off the merkaba of the activating individual. After the disaster which destroyed Atlantis, the ascended masters disseminated to three principal points in the globe: to Egypt and the area of the pyramids; to Meso-America, the land of the Incas; and to the Himalayas. These areas are key points in the energy-grid system. The Egyptian point is the male, the Maya/Inca point the female and the Himalayan is neutral. Generally, earth reverted to barbarianism until the Nefilim returned in the fourth century BCE and made connections again in the Middle East. Again, aspects of this story hark back to Chapter 3.

DRUNVALO MELCHIZEDEK

If you are anything like me, such a name as Drunvalo Melchizedek immediately presses all your derision buttons. It sounds unbelievably 'pose-y' and full of New Age scam. Several of my friends who devote a lot of their lives to shamanic development have avoided anything to do with this teacher simply because of his name. And yet I found myself thinking, just how might a being from a higher dimension seek to make contact with us in a credible way? Isn't it possible, that in getting down to our level, he or she might get it wrong and come across as patronising or just silly? If you have ever tried to get down to the level of a child you will know what I mean. It is easy to strike the wrong note and evoke nothing but scorn. How much more difficult it must be to descend from the higher dimensions down into the murk and travail that is our daily life.

As it happens, 'Melchizedek' is a generic term for ascended masters who are our teachers. Drunvalo has come down from the thirteenth dimension to act as a catalyst for the transition of our consciousness. He is here to teach sacred geometry and certain breathing patterns to activate the merkaba and to achieve unity consciousness. It is certainly not the place of this book to discuss Melchizedek's teaching, and I have not undertaken such training myself. My background is more of the instinctual 'wise woman' and pagan, although this may turn out to have more in common with Melchizedek's teachings than is obvious. At the moment I cannot say. This chapter, indeed, is not about what I know but about what I am musing. However, I have seen Drunvalo Melchizedek on video and he impressed me as a man with no ego. This view was endorsed by others watching – all sensible women with jobs, children (or grandchildren) and busy lives. He appeared to have no axe to grind and not even to consider whether or not he was being taken seriously, speaking in a matter-of fact way about the information contained in this chapter. He did not have the hypnotic charisma of one who is fired by his own vision, but more the glow of someone who is holding up a lamp, and he has humour. His teachings are generally available in the Flower of Life workshops, detailed earlier.

As we have seen, in the Great Pyramid are situated the King's Chamber and the Queen's Chamber, so named because of their differing shapes. The roof of the King's Chamber is flat, and Muslims buried men under flat roofs, where the Queen's Chamber has a pitched roof, like the roofs under which they buried their women. According to Drunvalo these chambers have nothing at all to do with burial and were used solely for initiation. After 12 years of Left Eye of Horus training, concerning the emotional body, and 12 more of Right Eye of Horus training in unity consciousness, final initiation took place in the Great Pyramid, beginning in a passage underneath it, ascending

to the King's Chamber and then to the Queen's. Under the Great Pyramid, the energy spiral going through the centre of the earth and the Halls of Amenti can be encountered. Here there is a tunnel, still extant, that seems to go nowhere, and this is where this energy spiral can be encountered. In fact, it is a four-dimensional space, so that what you think becomes real. Tourists have died because they brought into being their greatest fears, and many strange things have happened, so the tunnel has been closed to visitors.

The energy encountered here is called 'black light' in contrast to the 'white light' of the King's chamber. This chamber appears to be inexplicably off-centre, but the sarcophagus is positioned so that someone lying in it would experience the white light spiral passing straight through his or her pineal gland, or 'third eye'. The white crystalline powder found by archaelologists in the King's Chamber corresponds to a chemical secreted by the pituitary gland when a person is in a state of deep meditation, that condenses to a powder. A lot of this powder was found in the King's Chamber, suggesting the initiation of many persons. After spending three and a half days in a state of expanded consciousness, the initiate would then be brought to the Queen's Chamber to be stabilised and settled into the newly attained Christ-consciousness.

THE SPHINX AND THE HALL OF RECORDS

The wisdom and patterns of sacred geometry were passed on orally and inscribed only in one piece. That place is in a long passageway beneath the Great Pyramid. This leads to the Hall of Records, underneath the Sphinx. Here, the memory of the earth is preserved, through the times of pole shift and cataclysm, from a past too distant to be imagined. As we saw, the psychic Edgar Cayce foretold that this would be found under the right paw of the Sphinx. Graham Hancock and Robert Bauval have speculated that the location may be under investigation by a team of official Egyptologists who are the only people allowed near the Sphinx. Thoth and Drunvalo have said that the head of the Sphinx will fall off and that a large golden sphere will be found in the neck, and that this sphere is a time capsule. Currently, everything is being done by the authorities to hold the Sphinx together, after all, it is the most impressive of all ancient structures. Thoth has stated that things were so staged, at higher dimensional levels, so that the Hall of Records would be discovered before 1990, and it seems unclear whether or not this has, in fact, happened. If so, it has been kept quiet. The prediction of Thoth was that 148 sets of three people would attempt to enter the Hall, until one of the sets, coming from the West, would open the door by making a sound with their voices. You will notice, once again, the importance of sound. Then the trio would encounter a spiral stairway leading to a room underground, which the Japanese already have the technical know-how to locate, so clearly that a clay pot can be detected in the corner. From here, three channels are available and the clay pot has the means to indicate the correct avenue. If the wrong avenue is chosen the person will die.

If you are one of the three chosen, you will encounter no problem. A long passageway, lit only by a luminosity in the air, will show etchings of the chromosomal patterns associated with Christ-consciousness, the first of which is the flower of life. At the end of the passage exists a room containing proof of the existence of life on the planet for the last 5,500,000 years. At the front of this chamber is a stone at the top of which is a physical marker for each of the individuals who are admitted, an image or photograph and a name, plus a date, which will be the actual date of the day in question. Thoth was going to be there to meet these people but, unless this has actually happened, someone else will now meet them. Each of the explorers will be allowed to take an object out of the chamber. Here, information is stored on many dimensional levels and these are not merely physical objects.

POLE SHIFT AND CHANGE IN CONSCIOUSNESS

It is unclear exactly what the function of these three explorers and the artefacts they discover may be, but this doubtless has a material part to play in the coming changes that are foretold for our planet. The Sphinx and the pyramids are constructed in the way they are because only objects that are totally natural and in harmony with the earth itself can possibly survive such upheaval. This would, in part, seem to explain why the Giza complex has so many resonances with earth and cosmos. Concerning pole shift and our consciousness, the news, according to Drunvalo Melchizedek, is good.

Apparently, our planet is due to make the most massive jump in consciousness that has ever been made and there are beings from many parts of the universe and many dimensional levels gathering to witness the transition. Pole shift is associated with massive destruction and movement in consciousness of survivors, usually downwards, but for us the way is up, this time. Because of the planetary grid that has been set up and the work being done by ascended masters and others, the ride could be smooth and organic. People in their millions may suddenly spontaneously recall the merkaba and be able to use it. Thus, we can hopefully all make the move smoothly and harmoniously.

And so we have an alternative view of the meaning of the pyramids and the Sphinx. Writers such as Hancock, Bauval and Colin Wilson are suggesting the powerful symbolic meanings of these monuments concerning the awakening of humans into a new, enlightened state of being, or the discovery of old wisdom, or both and, in this respect, a key to some sort of breakthrough may be found on the Giza plateau. Ancient and modern, analytical and imaginative unite to form an entirely fresh and brilliant perspective. The much more extreme view defines the pyramids as quite literal vehicles for change of consciousness, connected with extra-terrestrials, ascended masters and other dimensions and associated with sacred geometry, that has definable though far-fetched application.

SUMMING UP

In the search for my 'open secret' we have travelled through some well-substantiated, alternative archaeology through to the badlands of the speculative and unproven, peopled with space travellers and immortals. You could be forgiven for reacting with a snigger of disbelief, but ask yourself again, 'what if?'. If you have ever felt that our present view of reality was incomplete, is it not possible that there is something of value here? It is left to us all to make up our own minds and to explore more deeply, if we choose. So much of this intriguing material is associated with the Giza plateau and its majestic relics. In a sense, the implications, from both ends of the spectrum, are similar, although admittedly to a vastly different degree. I believe they amount to this – that we are capable of more, or greater things. A unity is also implied, between human and human, human and cosmos, the same living thread weaving through all. We are searching to grasp the end of this thread and our awareness is changing. Perhaps the important factor is that we are *aware* that our awareness is changing. As David Elkington described it to me.

> *We are going through a unique change of awareness because we are aware of the change that is happening, and this is creating a 'stargate'. We have*

> *suddenly all become aware of the mystery, but in a sense we don't want it explained. We need to face the fact and be prepared to enter the labyrinth.*

I would go so far as to say that it cannot be explained, because that would be to reduce everything to the restricted mind-space of that old left brain. The glimpses I have of this 'mystery' fill me with hope and excitement. However, if we do not feel willing and able to enter the 'labyrinth'; if we entertain some indisputably reasonable doubts about the mere existence of any 'mystery' we can still ask again – about our history, our origins, our potentials and our future. And we can keep asking.

8 FOOTSTEPS INTO THE TWENTY-FIRST CENTURY

You cannot fight against the future. Time is on our side.

WILLIAM GLADSTONE, REFORM BILL SPEECH, 1866

For I dipt into the future, far as human eye could see,
Saw the Vision of the world, and all the wonder that would be.

TENNYSON, *LOCKSLEY HALL*

Prophecies and feared catastrophes notwithstanding, it seems to me that the principle point about the millennium is that it turns our attention to ourselves and our society, our achievements and potentials, and emphasises the need for a change within us. Our genetic structures mutate at the rate of only half a per cent every hundred years, meaning that most of us still, in a sense, belong in the Stone Age. However, the competitive 'me' consciousness that produced the Iron Age and centuries of conquest and 'progress', while having served us in some ways, is plain outdated. Unless we can outgrow this, there is a real chance that our survival instincts will prove self-defeating as we kill the goose that lays the golden eggs and stick to warrior motifs that are past their sell-by-date. Bullying by market forces and monetarism is simply antediluvian. The call for a new consciousness may be muted, but it is insistent.

We do not even need to look forward or backward to some 'Golden Age' for a model of co-operative and supportive living, for this is actually quite well embodied for us by many indigenous peoples, and the Yequana Indians, of Southern America are one good example. Close bonding, acceptance, warmth and a happy, philosophical outlook that is infectious mean that these people do not regard life as a set of obstacles, but as something to be met joyfully. Tasks are undertaken smilingly, as joint ventures, and if someone does not wish to repair the roof of their hut, the other members of the community do it for them. Of course, it simply does not happen that an indigenous Yequana objects to such jobs, for they come naturally and everyone helps their neighbour when this becomes necessary. It is only when outsiders enter the picture that the tolerance and acceptance of the Yequana are thrown into relief. People are not left to fend for themselves but are cared for by the community and, while some healthy competition does exist, it does not destroy the supportive framework. Beneath this culture must lie a reality structure that is different from 'survival of the fittest' where the welfare of the one is the welfare of all. Basically, it's a state of mind. The example of the Yequana inspires faith in the human spirit and is living proof that humanitarianism is common sense. Their lifestyle has been used as a blueprint for alternative and enlightened parenting in *The Continuum Concept* by Jean Liedloff (Arkana, 1989). This is the sort of thing we are capable of and this is what we can rediscover and modify in a technological lifestyle.

If our Palaeolithic chromosomes need a push, they may get one from several sources. Changes in the upper atmospheric layers, some human-made, some natural, result in a greater amount of cosmic radiation falling on the surface of the planet, and this radiation causes mutation. We tend to think of mutation as a distortion, as things gone wrong, but mutation means change. In fact, in the best possible (although admittedly less likely) scenario, this radiation could be the evolutionary kick-start for which we are ready. Around 700,000 years in the past, a huge meteorite exploded over the Indian Ocean showering fragments over an immense area. At the same time the poles of the earth also reversed, meaning that the earth was temporarily without the usual magnetic field that acts as a protection against cosmic rays. Thus, the earth was bombarded by radiation. In *African Genesis* (Athenaeum, 1961) Robert Ardrey puts forward the theory that these cosmic rays were responsible for the 'brain explosion' – the fact that the human race now evolved more in half a million years than apparently in the previous three million. Another factor is the neutrino radiation emitted by supernovas. Neutrinos have been called 'the seeds of life' and are recognised by scientists as being instrumental in shaping evolution on the planet. The giant supernova in February 1987 flung out a hail of neutrinos (uncharged particles with zero mass when static) and radiation that probably affected each person on earth in what could be called a 'quickening', registered consciously by some and for others operating at an unconscious level. This seemed to coincide with prophecies of change in our times. In addition, there are the changes that we consciously foster in our wish to progress, for in increasing numbers people are recognising something has got to give, From many angles, the stage is set for a big move.

The coming alterations possible for humans have been defined in a variety of ways. Some foretell a huge and quite sudden change in all of us that lifts us to a higher dimension and totally alters our perception of reality in a way that is quite unimaginable; others speak in more concrete terms of a full connection and integration between the right and left halves of the brain, so that intuition dances in tandem with logic, making us more highly and completely aware. A new understanding between masculine and feminine, a greater internal balance and integration between the conscious mind and the 'forbidden' area of the 'shadow' of the personality – all these mean, in essence, unity. As far as I am concerned, we have to find our way back to the 'garden' – that blissful state of instinctual participation in life that some say existed many aeons ago; that state in which we knew so much, and yet did not feel the need to act, or even articulate, when our consciousness was intergalactic and our lives primitive. But now, in the words of T.S. Eliot,

We shall not cease from exploration
And the end of all our exploring
Will be to arrive where we started
And know the place for the first time

We can regain our sense of beauty, wonderment and oneness, while retaining our discriminative, analytical function. This seems paradoxical, and yet the appearance of paradox depends, perhaps, on perspective, and this perspective is something we can rise above, on the wings of evolution. We can hope that humankind is on the brink of realising full potential and that the intelligence and nobility which we tend rather conceitedly to claim, will, in fact, truly be ours.

Of course, this can all sound far-flung. Having read this far you may well be asking 'Yes, but what do I *do*?'. Feeling that change is afoot you may want to be a creative part of it. This can be accomplished in so many ways, outer and inner, abstract and concrete, and each of these may be as valuable as the others. In the end, all choices are entirely yours and all I can offer are pointers. Let us start with the inner way.

INNER PROGRESS

By 'inner' progress I do not mean, of course, simply mental improvement which can be achieved by embarking on almost any course of study, but something that is intended to expand awareness which is rather a different thing. Real inward expansion is almost inexpressible, but that doesn't matter. There are many ways you can use to approach the subject. Above all, you may choose to be open, not rejecting anything because you do not understand it at present. You may wish simply to practise meditation and to embark on a routine of meditating. You may decide to get to know yourself better through counselling or analysis. Remember, whatever path you choose, good old routine is vital. We may despise people who are sticklers for routine, buy maybe there is wisdom hidden here, because routine is hard to get into at first, is deeply valuable when established and may be hard to retrieve when broken. Bad routines (i.e. bad habits) on the other hand are cursedly difficult to break. Routine is part of our unconscious programing. Examine yours. Do you wish to reprogram yourself? You can, if you wish. Start with something small that you have

decided upon and build from there. This is a real step in self-determinism, for the vast majority of us, for the vast majority of our lives, act automatically and thoughtlessly, taking the line of least resistance and failing to use the free will that we cherish.

You may be searching for a spiritual direction. Remember, what is important is what is right for you, where you find a sense both of belonging and inspiration. This does not even have to be clearly defined to anyone else. True religion is about a sense of the sacred, of being part – a meaningful part – of something greater than oneself. A quest for this may be your millenarian journey. If so, why put it off, or be put off by others?

Other inward skills may consist of training up your intuitive or clairvoyant faculties. As these improve, your outlook will change. Further Reading, at the end of this book, lists books that will get you started. The entire subject of self-development, self-expansion or spiritual quest is so vast that it can and does fill many books, and yet is intensely personal. What I can usefully say is that it is a first step to be open and to explore and that it is okay to start small. It's also okay to be confused, because we all are at times. The following Chinese saying is worth bearing in mind.

> *He that knows not, yet thinks that he knows, shun him, for he is a fool.*
> *He that knows not and knows that he knows not, offer him guidance, for he will learn.*
> *He that knows, and knows not that he knows, wake him for he is asleep.*
> *And he that knows, and knows that he knows, follow him, for he is wise.*

It is probably best to choose just one subject or direction, at first, and give up only after you have given it your best shot and decided it is not for you. That's not failure, it's the learning process. Then try something else. Naturally, gifts bring responsibilities and, as you grow, you will have more to give out. You may get a buzz out of this and feel proud of yourself and I think that is fine, in balance. Be honest with yourself. We all have egos. It is what pushes us onwards, giving us integration and focus and, like so many things, it is a good friend but a dangerous master.

You may choose to study one of the mantic, or predictive, arts which will also expand your intuitive faculties. As we examined earlier in this book, the purpose of the prophet is to warn, to encourage wisdom. Prediction is small-scale prophecy and, while many of us want to know simply what will happen, the purpose of the predictive arts is to enhance awareness in all directions, so resist being seduced by the need to be clever and 'right'. Most people who have sought to develop their intuition and expand their awareness agree that contact with nature is immensely beneficial in fostering this. For inward development, in my opinion it is hard to beat a routine of conscious relaxation, meditation and opening of the chakras. Again, plenty of instructions for this can be found in some of the books in Further Reading. Simply affirming repeatedly to yourself that you wish to become a creative part of the planetary evolution process will bring results and you may find you are shown ways to progress. Be aware of these signs, for life drops many hints. For example, you may have been thinking of doing yoga. Then you spot an advertisement for a class in a local store. You hesitate. Then a leaflet about the yoga class drops on your door mat. Get the message?

Finally, whatever direction you select, thinking of yourself as a cell of light, a resting place for spirit, can surely only be positive.

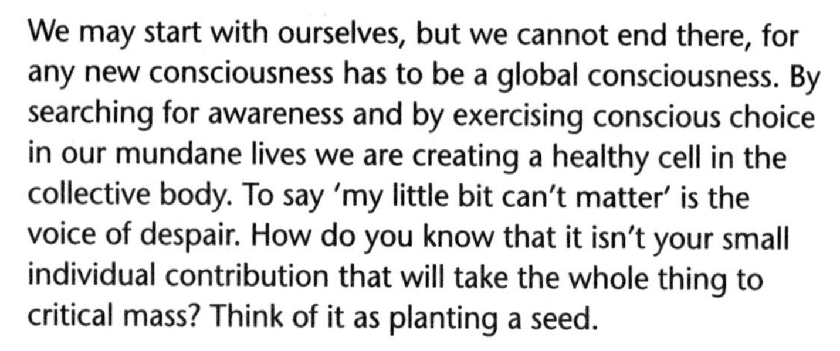

CITIZENSHIP OF THE NEW MILLENNIUM

We may start with ourselves, but we cannot end there, for any new consciousness has to be a global consciousness. By searching for awareness and by exercising conscious choice in our mundane lives we are creating a healthy cell in the collective body. To say 'my little bit can't matter' is the voice of despair. How do you know that it isn't your small individual contribution that will take the whole thing to critical mass? Think of it as planting a seed.

Unless you are prepared to mount your soap-box and lead the faithful to your version of the New Kingdom, your spiritual efforts for the global family are unlikely to be dramatic, but I believe we can all make a definite contribution to world peace. If there are international issues that cause concern – as usually is the case – why not simply light a candle for world peace, for the abolition of famine, or whatever? Make a basic affirmation such as 'Let there be peace' and visualise something simple, such as a handshake, or an abundance of bread. This goes by the old-fashioned name of prayer, as you may notice, but it is prayer that is focused by the imagination and needs no specific belief behind it. Involve family and friends, if they are willing. All over the world these efforts are slowly growing, gradually turning the tide, through human awareness and caring.

Start or join a group that promotes awareness of New Age subjects. Anything that raises the spiritual consciousness is a step in the right direction. Show respect for and defend the rights of any spiritual pathway or belief that is compatible with freedom and peace, even if you cannot share in it. Take part in celebrations of life, where you find them. Visualise the earth as a big, beautiful garden and the human race as one family, where diversity is honoured and quarrels settled before bedtime.

PRACTICAL CITIZENSHIP

We all know that our way of life is not sustainable and that the ecosystem is being inexorably damaged. Again, there may seem little point in unilateral action. However, we have to start somewhere. Your actions may give inspiration to others and they are an example of exercise of free choice. Not to exercise this is similar to not bothering to vote, when so many have died in the cause of universal suffrage. The purpose of the following checklist is not to cause guilt but to act as a memory-jerker. Doing a little bit is a start.

Recycling, reusing

Request not to have a bag when shopping; recycle tins, glass, paper, plastics; compost waste; purchase products that contain recycled materials; use a cloth rather than tissue paper where possible; buy loose and in bulk where possible; lobby local government to provide recycling facilities; pass on old clothes to charity.

Earth-friendly products

Use biodegradable, phosphate-free cleaning products; don't run the washing machine half full; fit a watersaving device to the toilet flush; take showers not baths; purchase *no* aerosols (CFCs are only half the story, others use butane as a propellant which is a 'greenhouse gas'); buy personal care products that are not tested on animals and have a preponderance of natural ingredients; purchase no tropical hardwood products that deplete the rainforests; use rechargeable batteries. Avoid weedkillers, chemical fertilisers and pesticides (organo-phosphates are harmful to humans, there is an aromatherapy cure for headlice, flea-ridden animals may have to live outside); buy organically grown, local produce where possible; become vegetarian, or largely so (eating lower down the biological chain results in the ingestion of fewer harmful substances and is far more ecologically sustainable. If you do not wish to be vegetarian, choose organic, humanely reared meat and cut meat consumption. (At the time of writing, in April 1998, the current major threat to our food is genetic modification, which amounts to an uncontrolled experiment with our bodies and with the food chain. You may wish to write letters of protest, if appropriate. Addresses and contacts for this and similar campaigns are sure to be available at your local wholefood shop.)

Conservation

Use low-energy light bulbs; insulate doors, windows and cavity walls; fit solar panels in the roof to provide power; turn the heating down two degrees and put on a sweater; buy energy-efficient appliances; turn off lights; re-use water (i.e. washing-up water for the garden); beware of appliances that are eternally on standby, such as remote-controlled televisions and video recorders where there is a time display (more trouble to reset of course, but it will help to cut your bill).

Transport

Fit a catalytic converter to your car; use an energy-efficient car; car share where possible; use a bike if you can (good exercise!); walk short distances; take public transport where possible; support the development of vehicles that do not need petrol, campaign for improvement in public transport, etc.

Positive action

Join or support an environmental organisation (some are listed in Resources at the end of this book); take an interest in local, environmental projects; plant a tree; hug a tree; defend local areas of special value or beauty from development and road-building.

Money

Make sure the organisation you work for has sound ecological values and, if possible, that it invests ethically – if not, move elsewhere when you can; work for an organisation that is explicitly environment-active if that is possible for you; find out about the investment policies of your bank, building society, credit card, pension fund and consider changing if it supports the arms trade or other unethical investment.

THE SHADOW

A positive attitude is productive, but one of the principal drawbacks in much that is called 'New Age' is that the shadow is not always sufficiently addressed or acknowledged. With 'love and light' on everyone's lips it is tempting to believe that we can simply rise above all that is base and unpleasant, but that is just kidding ourselves. As we progress in our awareness and development, walking towards what we see as the light, we must not forget that behind us, always attached to us, follows our shadow. Shadow can be defined as an absense of light and we may believe that light can always drive out darkness. However, only in sterile space can there be no shadow. Wherever there exists the fertility of diversity, wherever there is growth – in short, wherever there is life – there will always be something on which the light can fall and that will always create a shadow.

The shadow is a powerful metaphor for an aspect of the human mind, defined and described by C.G. Jung. Our 'shadow' is all that we repress as being unacceptable, horrible, fearful, all that we will not allow into the light of consciousness. The shadow stands on the threshold of the unconscious mind and we must encounter it, before we can come to know ourselves deeply. Like so many similar concepts, the shadow has many levels, many aspects, and perhaps can never be completely encapsulated, for it is awesome and mysterious. However, the shadow in each of us and in society at large must be addressed if we are to evolve as individuals and even survive as a species.

In the shadow of each of us resides all the traits that we abhor in ourselves and that we strenuously pretend do not exist. The shadow will contain things that were repressed in childhood, but we cannot blame our parents for our shadows, for the shadow is part of our destiny. We may tell ourselves we want to get to know ourselves, but no one really wants to know their shadow, because it is plain nasty. Often, a key to the shadow is what we most hate about other people. For instance, I really hate dogmatism and I have to admit to some pockets of the dogmatic in myself. But that is much too glib to be more than a flitting shade. The real shadow causes burning shame and self-disgust, and for this reason we project our shadow on to other people, because it is much more comfortable. Whenever we find ourselves saying 'I can't stand . . .' we would do well to pause for a moment to ask ourselves what this says about us. This can be so unacceptable at first that we may reject it out of hand – 'Surely that is rubbish? I would never be, do or say such a thing', etc. It is probably absolutely true that we would 'never be' child molestors, muggers or whatever. None the less, if we have a special hatred, something that is out of proportion, then this is a tell-tale sign, not of what we would necessarily do, but of something that is within us. Facing our darkness is not about acting it out, but to be aware of it.

This is not, and never will be, an easy matter, and the shadow can probably never be fully faced, or integrated. Certainly it cannot be driven away by 'the light' for that would result in an even deeper shadow somewhere else. The best we can probably do with our shadow is to face it as best we can, be aware of it, accept it as a nodding acquaintance – someone we wish lived on the other side of the country but cannot be expelled from our basement. The reason why the shadow is so important is that it lies at the cause of so many, if not all, conflicts, both personal and collective, and if we do not recognise it we become inexorably involved in fights, often to the death. The collective shadow of the Nazis rested upon the Jews, white people have hated black as a convenient embodiment of the shadow, people we 'love to hate' from soap-opera villains to Saddam Hussein carry our shadow. This doesn't mean that there are no malevolent or damaged people, but that we do not deal with such matters in a balanced, sensible fashion, because we are subconsciously involved in exterminating our own shadow. Peace between neighbours and nations depends at least upon acknowledging the shadow and, because this is so painful, it is a task we would far rather avoid, even sometimes to the point of death.

A FERTILE PLACE

As we seek to cultivate love and light in the new millennium, we cannot honestly avoid hatred and darkness. This doesn't mean, of course, that we act them out, but neither does it mean we seek to expunge them from within us. Rather we need to walk in acceptance and awareness. However, there also comes a point, I believe, where analysis of our shadow becomes unproductive and actually subtly plays into our shadowy bits (the shadow is like that!) meaning we become much less creative and, in effect, disappear up our own posterior! Lives can be mutilated in this way. For instance, preoccupation with facing the shadow and its expression in a relationship has resulted in more than one person whom I know remaining for far too long in what was a bad relationship, however you looked at

it, because they were trying to 'take back' and deal with the shadowy parts of themselves that they were projecting on to the partner. Of course, this is noble and necessary but, while you are trying to face the fact that you may hate all men (or women), and why this may be, you may be obscuring the fact that your partner really is behaving hatefully. As with so many things, the 'middle way' of the Chinese sages is to be recommended.

'Love' and 'light' are buzz words of the New Age, and we have seen that they beg the question of the shadow. However, it is also trendy to 'face one's dark side' without perhaps quite appreciating what this entails. Sometimes this may result in a self-absorbed lifestyle that is not as creative as it might be. Many people also striving genuinely for self-awareness and acceptance of their less desirable qualities, are driven, none the less, by all the tired 'shoulds' and 'oughts' in another guise, aiming for universal love and in reality being old-fashioned martyrs. Surely this cannot be the way to the unity consciousness, the loving consciousness that we have called Christ-consciousness? Christ-consciousness, I feel, comes through development and evolution, and is not created by guilt and dogma. Neither does it necessarily have anything at all to do with Christian observances. You can't pretend love when you do not feel it, and if you do not feel it, this will out, in some fashion. Christ-consciousness, in effect, is not about what you do, but what you are. Once achieved, it is no ordinary state and has nothing to do with petty self abasement or false humility. It is, in essence, love and it is achieved through love. This love starts with ourselves, being able to love and accept ourselves in entirety – something that almost all of us have been taught not to do – and extending from there. This also involves a creative use of the imagination, the small starters for which we looked at earlier, for imagination can lift us to new possibilities, great and small, and show us new meanings and new visions.

The shadow is also an area of 'compost' for this is a fertile place, where a lot of our power gets bogged down. If we will make attempts to address our shadow, we can find this frees up a lot of our energy and makes us more creative. The shadow isn't always composed of the truly undesirable, by any definition, for we may fear our power and our qualities as much as our vices. This matter was addressed by Nelson Mandela in his inaugural address in 1994, and this I choose as my anthem for the millennium:

Our deepest fear is not that we are inadequate.
Our deepest fear is that we are powerful beyond measure.
It is our light, not our darkness that most frightens us.

We ask ourselves, who am I to be brilliant, gorgeous, talented and fabulous?
Actually, who are you not to be?

You are a child of God.
Your playing small doesn't serve the world.
There's nothing enlightened about shrinking so that other people won't feel insecure around you.

We were born to make manifest the glory of God that is within us.
It's not just in some of us, it's in everyone!

And as we let our light shine we unconsciously give other people permission to do the same.
As we are liberated from our own fear, our presence automatically liberates others.

FURTHER READING

Nathaniel Altman, *The Palmistry Workbook*, Aquarian, 1984

Baigent, Campion and Harvey, *Mundane Astrology*, Aquarian, 1985

Robert Bauval and Graham Hancock, *Keeper of Genesis*, Mandarin, 1997

Charles Berlitz, *Atlantis, The Lost Continent Revealed*, Macmillan, 1984

John Blofield, *I Ching, the Book of Change*, Unwin, 1976

Harold Bloom, *Omens of Millennium*, Fourth Estate, 1996

Erika Cheetham, *The Final Prophecies of Nostradamus*, Futura Macdonald, 1990

Michael Craft, *Alien Impact*, St Martin's Press, 1996

Richard Craze, *Feng Shui – A Complete Guide*, Hodder & Stoughton, 1997

Scott Cunningham, *Encyclopaedia of Crystal, Gem and Metal Magic*, Llewellyn, 1994

Timothy Ferris, *The Whole Shebang, A State of the Univere(s) Report*, Weidenfeld & Nicolson, 1997

Frieda Fordham, *An Introduction to Jung's Psychology*, Pelican, 1985

Bob Frissell, *Nothing In This Book Is True, But It's Exactly How Things Are*, Frog Ltd, 1994

Shakti Gawain, *Creative Visualisation*, Whatever Publishing, 1985

Adrian Gilbert and Maurice Cotterell, *The Maya Prophecies*, Element, 1996

Liz Greene, *The Outer Planets and Their Cycles*, CRCS Publications, 1983

Margaret Gullan-Whur, *What Your Handwriting Reveals*, Aquarian, 1986

Graham Hancock, *Fingerprints of the Gods: A Quest for the Beginning and the End*, Mandarin, 1997
Charles Hapgood, *Maps of the Ancient Sea Kings*, Turnstone, 1979
Louise Hay, *You Can Heal Your Life*, Eden Grove, 1988
Arthur Koestler, *The Sleepwalkers, A History of Man's Changing Vision of the Universe*, Penguin, 1984
Emily Peach, *The Tarot Workbook*, Aquarian, 1984
Darryl Reanney, *The Death of Forever*, Souvenir, 1991
James Redfield, *The Celestine Prophecy*, Bantam, 1995
R.J. Stewart, *The Elements of Prophecy*, Element, 1991
Moria Timms, *Prophecies To Take You Into the Twenty-First Century*, Thorsons, 1996
Max Toth and Greg Nielsen, *Pyramid Power*, Thorsons, 1988
Colin Wilson, *Mysteries*, Grafton, 1986
Colin Wilson, *From Atlantis to the Sphinx*, Virgin, 1997
Holy Bible, Authorised King James Version, Oxford University Press

Caduceus Magazine, Issue 38
38 Russell Terrace, Leamington Spa, Warwickshire,
CV31 1HE, UK.
E-mail: caduceus@oryx.demon.co.uk

Quest Magazine, amateur astronomy and earth sciences
Top Events Ltd, PO Box 1008, Chester, CH3 9AE, UK.
Tel: +44 (0)1829 770884

A Beginner's Guide series, published by Hodder & Stoughton

This is a series of compact books designed to explain the basics of a wide range of esoteric 'New Age' subjects. Of particular relevance to the subject matter in this book are *Witchcraft, Paganism, The Goddess, Shamanism, Pagan Gods for Today's Man, Earth Mysteries, The Magic and Mystery of Trees, Your Psychic Powers, Mediumship, Feng Shui, Chakras, I Ching, Astrology, Tarot, Runes, Gems and Crystals, Numerology, Numerology and Relationships, Reiki, Palmistry, Graphology*, and others. A full list appears on the last page of this book.

RESOURCES

The Club of Budapest
Foundation Hungary, H – 1014 Budapest, Szentharomsag ter 6, Hungary
Tel/Fax: 0036 1175 1885
E-mail: H13471las@ella.hu

The Club of Budapest International
12a Thurloe Street, London, SW7 2ST, UK.
Tel: +44 (0)171 700 2333
E-mail: 106100.2404@compuserve.com
Website: http://newciv.org/ClubofBudapest

Trees of Time and Place – A New Initiative for a New Millennium
96 Victoria Street, London, SW1E 5JW, UK
Tel: +44 (0)345 078 139

Centre for Alternative Technology
Canolfan Y Dechnoleg Amgen, Machynlleth Powys, SY20 9AZ, UK
Tel: +44 (0)1654 702400.
Courses and publications.

Faculty of Astrological Studies
Ref T. Moorey, BM7470, London, WC1N 5XX, UK
Tel: +44 (0) 7000 790145 (24-hr answering)
E-mail: info@astrology.org.uk
Website: http://www.astrology.org.uk

The Pagan Federation
BM Box 7097, London, WC1N 3XX, UK
E-mail: Secretary@paganfed.demon.co.uk
Website: http://www.paganfed.demon.co.uk

Pagan Alliance for Ozzies
PO Box 823, Bathurst, NSW 2795, Australia

Green Egg magazine for Eco-Paganism
Box 1542, Ukiah, CA 95482, USA

Hecate's Loom, dynamic pagan magazine,
Box 5206, Station B, Victoria
BC V8R 6N4
Canada

Positive News
A quarterly newspaper bringing you the latest good news about ecology, health, environmental projects, humanitarian issues and lots more.
The Six Bells, Church St, Bishop's Castle, SY9 5AA, UK
Tel: +44 (0)1588 630 121
E-mail: positive.news@btinternet.com
Website: www.oneworld.org/positive_news

American Forestry Association
Tel: Global Releaf (202) 667 3300

Forests Forever
Tel: America (707) 462 2370

American Rainforest Action Network
Tel: (415) 398 4404

Earthwise Products ECO-HOME
4344 Russell Avenue, Los Angeles, CA 90027, USA

Global Family
112 Jordan Avenue, San Anselmo, CA 94960, USA
Tel: (415) 453 7600

Earth Link Foundation
PO Box 677, Biron Bay, NSW 2481, Australia

***Planetary Connections* International Newspaper** – linking those worldwide who are dedicated to bringing the vision of a new era into reality.
Spiritual Growth Foundation, 7 Green Oaks Road, Asheville, NC 28804, USA

Friends of the Earth
26–28 Underwood Street, London, N1 7JQ, UK

DRAGON eco-pagan action group
3 Sanford Walk, New Cross, London, UK

Greenpeace
Canonbury Villas, London, N1 2PN, UK

Other titles in this series

Astral Projection
Astrology
Astrology and Health
Becoming Prosperous
Chakras
Channelling
Chinese Horoscopes
Dowsing
Dream Interpretation
Earth Mysteries
Enlightenment
Feng Shui
Freeing Your Intuition
Gems and Crystals
The Goddess
Graphology
The Healing Powers of Plants
Herbs for Magic and Ritual
I Ching
Interpreting Signs and Symbols
The Language of Flowers
Love Signs
The Magic and Mystery of Trees
Meditation
Mediumship
The Moon and You
Numerology
Numerology and Relationships
Pagan Gods for Today's Man
Paganism
Palmistry
Qabalah
Reiki
Reincarnation and You
Runes

Shamanism
Some Traditional African Beliefs
Spiritual Healing
Star Signs
Tantric Sexuality
Tarot
Visualisation
Witchcraft
Working With Colour
Your Psychic Powers